Jump-start Your SOC Analyst Career

A Roadmap to Cybersecurity Success

Tyler Wall
Jarrett Rodrick

Apress®

Jump-start Your SOC Analyst Career: A Roadmap to Cybersecurity Success

Tyler Wall
Braselton, GA, USA

Jarrett Rodrick
Melissa, TX, USA

ISBN-13 (pbk): 978-1-4842-6903-9
https://doi.org/10.1007/978-1-4842-6904-6

ISBN-13 (electronic): 978-1-4842-6904-6

Managing Director, Apress Media LLC: Welmoed Spahr
Acquisitions Editor: Susan McDermott
Development Editor: Laura Berendson
Coordinating Editor: Rita Fernando

Cover designed by eStudioCalamar

Distributed to the book trade worldwide by Springer Science+Business Media New York, 1 New York Plaza, New York, NY 10004. Phone 1-800-SPRINGER, fax (201) 348-4505, e-mail orders-ny@springer-sbm.com, or visit www.springeronline.com. Apress Media, LLC is a California LLC and the sole member (owner) is Springer Science + Business Media Finance Inc (SSBM Finance Inc). SSBM Finance Inc is a **Delaware** corporation.

For information on translations, please e-mail booktranslations@springernature.com; for reprint, paperback, or audio rights, please e-mail bookpermissions@springernature.com.

Apress titles may be purchased in bulk for academic, corporate, or promotional use. eBook versions and licenses are also available for most titles. For more information, reference our Print and eBook Bulk Sales web page at http://www.apress.com/bulk-sales.

Any source code or other supplementary material referenced by the author in this book is available to readers on GitHub via the book's product page, located at www.apress.com/978-1-4842-6903-9. For more detailed information, please visit http://www.apress.com/source-code.

Printed on acid-free paper

This book is dedicated to our wives, Heidi and Stacey.

Table of Contents

About the Authors

Tyler Wall is an accomplished security professional with years of experience in security operations and engineering that includes presently serving remotely as a Senior Security Engineer in Silicon Valley. He has led Security Operations Centers for global enterprises. His current focus is enabling Security Operations Centers to continuously mature by the adoption of security automation. Tyler's education includes a Master of Science in Cybersecurity Management, CISSP, CEH, CFSR, LRPA, Security+, Network+, and A+. He enjoys long golf cart rides in Braselton, GA, with his wife and son.

Jarrett Rodrick is the SOC Team Lead and Senior Information Security Analyst for VMware, the global leader in visualization technology. He's a retired Cyber Network Defender and Cyber Warfare Specialist from the US Army and has over 8 years of Defensive Cyber Operations experience working with the Army's Cyber Protection Brigade. Jarrett's time with the Cyber Protection Brigade has provided him with the skills needed to fight in today's cyberwar. Jarrett's cybersecurity certifications include GSEC, GCED, GCIH, GCIA, GCFE, GCFA, GSNA, GRID, GCUX, and GSTRT. Jarrett lives in Melissa, TX, with his wife and family and enjoys researching new and innovative technologies.

About the Contributors

Anand Purohit has been working in IT for over 15 years with the past 8 years focused on Technology and Cloud Strategy, Architecture, and Governance. He has held various executive roles within consulting, healthcare, and financial services working closely with peers in cybersecurity, risk, and compliance while transforming organizations' technology operating model using cloud (public, private, or hybrid). Anand graduated from Stevens Institute of Technology and now lives in Atlanta with his wife and son.

Jason Tunis is a Lead Security Operations Center analyst at Aegon with over 12 years of cybersecurity experience. He spends his time primarily focused on incident response, cyber threat intelligence, and security automation. Over the past 2 years, Jason has helped to build a highly skilled Security Operations Center. Jason lives in the Midwest with his wife and three children.

About the Technical Reviewer

 **Mark Furman** received his MBA from Ohio University and a Bachelor of Science in Information Technology from Purdue University. He has worked in the IT and cybersecurity field for over 19 years. Some of his accomplishments include writing and publishing a book on virtualization, participating as a technical editor for books, starting a successful cybersecurity program at a technical college, and launching a business incubator and makerspace. Currently, Mark is in the process of launching a new cybersecurity company called Kaldara Security.

Acknowledgments

First, I would like to acknowledge Apress for understanding the vision of this book: to make the impossible possible.

I would also like to acknowledge my employer VMware for the time and creative space to express my ideas. Additionally, I would like to acknowledge my leadership chain for their input concerning this book. VMware is a terrific company, and I believe in EPIC2 values which include community, the very cornerstone of this book.

I would like to humbly thank and acknowledge the few influential people in my life. My wife, Heidi. I would also like to thank my father, Peter. My mother and stepfather, Karen and Kenny. Sister and brother, Ginny and Lew. My friends, Steven C., Stephen S., Spencer R., Frank F., Andy W., Fred S., Dwight F., Philip S., Sam C., Chris P., Reese and Mike W., Daniel W., and Corey Milford and the Milford Team. I would like to thank my mother-in-law, Lori, and her mother Mary. I would like to extend that gratitude to my sister-in-law and her husband Shuvo. I would like to show thanks to my cousins Justin, Alan, Trey, Dana, and Michael and their kids. I would like to acknowledge my uncle, Edd. Lastly and in conclusion, I would like to thank my uncle, Chuck, for his most honorable service to this country and our family.

—Tyler Wall

First and most important, I'd like to thank my beautiful and loving wife, Stacey. Your constant supply of love and patience has provided me with the needed support to become the Cyber professional I am today. Thank you!

ACKNOWLEDGMENTS

I'd also like to thank the countless Soldiers and Army Leaders I've had the pleasure to learn from in my 16-year career. From my Drill Sergeants at Fort Knox to the Senior Officers at the Cyber Protection Brigade, you've all played a pivotal role in my development. Thank you!

Finally, I'd like to thank VMware, for taking a chance on a soon-to-retire Soldier and offering me a career outside of the Army. I truly couldn't have asked for a better company to work for. Thank you!

—Jarrett Rodrick

Introduction

Welcome to the wonderful world of *Jump-start Your SOC Analyst Career*!
You picked this book up because you want to get into the action! Into the
money! Into the challenges that lie ahead! We will tell you how wonderful
and rewarding this career is, but first let us say something about infosec.
If you get into the cybersecurity industry and you aren't connected to
the community, you are missing out. There are all kinds of micro infosec
communities and communities for special groups of people, but in
contrast there are communities that want to include everyone. There are
extremely esoteric communities filled with mystery and secrets, there are
communities for just CISOs and communities for just engineers, there is a
military community, communities for Bill and Bob, communities for the
government sector, a community of breakers and makers alike... if there
is only one common trait that people coming into security want, it is a
sense of community - and infosec has it! It is really hard to relate to people
in the normal world sometimes, especially if you are starting out and
keyboarding alone. We promise you there are many other people that want
to keyboard alone next to you. It happens all the time at conferences! There
are so many amazing people in the community, and sometimes they don't
always get along, but in 3–6 months, it will be like it never happened. Our
goal for this book is to get you in the chair in the SOC you dream about and
open your eyes that no matter who you are, cybersecurity is for you.

This book will cover what you need to know that we have deemed to
be important to know as a SOC analyst. There are a lot of open jobs in
cybersecurity, but there are also a lot of candidates that want those jobs.
The challenge is that there are not a lot of the right kind of candidates to fill
them. We explain to you what the right kind of candidate is and give you

the knowledge to prepare you for interviews. We can't promise to take you from technical zero to hero in the pages of this book. As an author I want you to trust me, and I will tell you how to be successful with this book, but you need to have a baseline of technical skills. Ideally by the point you pick up this book, you will have been learning IT skills for a while. The combined contributions of the creators of this book, Tyler Wall and Jarrett Rodrick, and chapter authors Anand Purohit and Jason Tunis, are orchestrated to give you, the reader, the advantage. Ending this book are five stories from people who have traversed the path of a SOC analyst.

The roadmap to cybersecurity success is long, and it's not an easy road at times. It isn't a straight vertical path for some either. It winds, it narrows, and it goes all over the place. To be successful in cybersecurity can mean a lot of things to a lot of people. For some that might mean holding the torch and power of a CISO, but if you really think hard about that path, it may not make sense for you. There are technical professionals that make more than a CISO, and their jobs are much more stable. Their heads aren't on a chopping block every time something goes bad. That is not to say that being a CISO and leading a security team isn't rewarding; I just illustrate the example to explain that paths and end goals are different from geek to geek according to personal aspirations, but the very first step to a rewarding career is always the same: getting a foot into this industry. Out of all the steps in cybersecurity, it is the most important. The foundation of a cybersecurity career can happen in the very first year as a SOC analyst. The first year as a SOC analyst is very overwhelming, and like drinking through a fire hose, expect to be satisfied but extremely uncomfortable. What is in this book will help you start your career as a SOC analyst and empower you to launch on day one.

Get ready for a rewarding career in cybersecurity..., and on day one, pick a good chair.

Puzzle Challenge

The **Illuminati Party**, creators of Raitlin's Challenge, present a puzzle
for your entertainment pleasure. The intent is to challenge the readers
of this book while raising funds in support of projects and research
facilitated by the National Upcycled Computing Collective, Inc., a 501(c)(3)
Nonprofit Organization (EIN 82-1177433) as determined by the Internal
Revenue Service with a National Taxonomy of Exempt Entities (NTEE)
U41 classification as a Computer Science, Technology and Engineering,
Research Institute.

Become a monthly supporting member today by visiting https://www.
nuccinc.org/donate.

Enjoy this little trip down the rabbit's hole.

Kwtv ko ukng vp qqq eqxp vig tbdcku-iqmg.

ivurt://ikqrjvz.nkogsxbnmwy.dqn

National Upcycled Computing Collective, Inc.

CHAPTER 1

The Demand for Cybersecurity and SOC Analysts

In this chapter we'll discuss the demand for cybersecurity professionals at three different levels, starting with the demand for cybersecurity workers, then address the demand of cybersecurity analysts and, finally, the demand for security operations center (SOC) analysts.

Cybersecurity During a Crisis

Early in 2020, the world began suffering from a viral pandemic known as COVID-19. The world shut down, and people were ordered to shelter in place in their homes. Many jobs were lost or furloughed until the quarantine was lifted, but many employers were able to transition to a "work from home" structure. Internet service providers (ISPs) saw long and enduring spikes in traffic, and the demand for videoconferencing soared to new heights. The United States Department of Homeland Security designated cybersecurity personnel as an essential workforce for continued infrastructure viability, and the need for cybersecurity workers is higher than ever. During this period, there was already a shortage of

© Tyler Wall and Jarrett Rodrick 2021
T. Wall and J. Rodrick, *Jump-start Your SOC Analyst Career*,
https://doi.org/10.1007/978-1-4842-6904-6_1

nearly 500,000 cybersecurity jobs in the United States alone, and the industry needed to grow by 62% to meet the current demand.[1]

> *Advanced Persistent Threat groups are using the COVID-19 pandemic as part of their cyber operations.*
>
> —US Dept. Homeland Security[2]

Having a current shortage in the cybersecurity workforce combined with a crisis such as the COVID-19 pandemic, a cyberwar, or any other emergency increases the demand for cybersecurity workers. The shortage of cyber workers gets even worse, and the cybersecurity workforce is drained even further. There is no solution but to work longer and harder. Cybersecurity workers' physical and mental health takes a toll as the stress and hours worked increase. There is not a fast fix or solution for training new cybersecurity workers, so the result is an extra-taxed workforce.

During the 2020 COVID-19 pandemic, the world rushed to continue to be productive while working at home. While the US government shut down businesses everywhere except those deemed as "essential" for some time, cybersecurity was one of these professions considered essential, and the already high demand for skilled workers grew overnight.[3]

What did the industries learn from the pandemic? COVID-19 proved that a very large workforce could be productive while working remotely. For years, US companies have taken steps to be more environmentally friendly. Whether it's sustainable power for their warehouses, recycling programs, or alternative fuel for delivery vehicles, around the world

---

[1] www.isc2.org/Research/Workforce-Study
[2] www.us-cert.gov/ncas/alerts/aa20-099a
[3] https://workingnation.com/covid-19-cybersecurity-and-it-workers-are-essential-in-demand-employees/

thousands of companies are embracing sustainable resources. Now that an at-home workforce is feasible, we believe companies will embrace this as an opportunity to decrease greenhouse emissions and increase employee happiness.

Demand for Cybersecurity Analysts

Today, we find ourselves in a global cyberwar. Every industry, in every country, is actively targeted by cyber criminals, state-sponsored hackers, and companies engaging in corporate espionage. That might sound like the plot to a low-budget movie starring your favorite 1990s action star, but the truth is everyone's a target. Even more troubling is the fact that it didn't start in 2020; this has been going on for decades. It's only been in the last 5 years that companies have identified the need for higher investments in cybersecurity.

High-profile compromises over the last 10 years have served a hard lesson for industries globally. In November 2014, Sony Pictures Entertainment announced they were the victim of a data breach. Analysts from *Reuters.com* estimated the compromise would cost Sony more than $75 million in recovery costs and lost revenue. More recently, the Capital One breach in August 2019 resulted in the theft of 100 million consumer credit applications. Attacks like these two have driven home the requirement for a dedicated cybersecurity workforce.

In fact, according to the US Bureau of Labor Statistics, the cybersecurity analyst occupation is projected to grow 32% from 2018 to 2028 in the United States, compared to 12% growth for other computer-related occupations and 5% total growth for all occupations.[4] One

---

[4]www.bls.gov/ooh/computer-and-information-technology/information-security-analysts.htm

significant benefit for those considering a move into cybersecurity is the relatively low bar for entry into the career field.

For decades the narrative has been "Go to college, earn a 4-year degree, get a career." This book will dedicate a chapter to covering the different entry paths into cybersecurity analyst positions. But for now, know that college is not the only path into a great career.

When companies embrace the need for cybersecurity, it usually begins with the Security Operations Center or SOC for short. The SOC is responsible for triage, investigation, and response to cybersecurity incidents. This concept is not new. Military and law enforcement agencies have been using Tactical Operations Centers (TOC) to coordinate operations during conflicts for decades. And like the TOC, the SOC serves as the Command and Control (C2) hub for first responders to cybersecurity incidents.

Definition   A cybersecurity incident is an adverse network event in an information system or network or the threat of the occurrence of such an event according to the SANS institute.[5]

The SOC isn't the only team dedicated to responding to cybersecurity incidents. Many companies have dedicated Digital Forensics and Incident Response (DFIR) teams to support the SOC in investigations and response. Usually, the DFIR team takes on long-term investigations from the SOC, allowing the SOC to focus on daily operations and live incidents. The skills required of DFIR analysts are very similar to SOC analysts, the most substantial difference being the focus around legal requirements for digital forensics and evidence collection. In truth, the majority of DFIR analysts begin their careers as SOC analysts.

---

[5]www.sans.org/security-resources/glossary-of-terms

Demand for SOC Analysts

Now that we've covered the general demand for cybersecurity analysts, let's get to the reason you picked up this book. Perhaps you're transitioning from the military into the civilian sector or a recent college graduate looking to get a foot in the door. Maybe you're in the information technology (IT) field already. Regardless, the purpose of this book is to prepare you to become a SOC analyst. Whether you wish to join a DFIR team or work your way up to management, the SOC analyst profession has the lowest barrier of entry for cybersecurity. Becoming a SOC analyst is an excellent strategic position to get your start in the industry.

When staffing a SOC, hiring managers have a few challenges that they continuously face. The most prevalent of those challenges is the revolving door of the SOC. After a SOC manager hires for an open position, it takes them several months to train the new analyst. Once training is complete, retention becomes a problem as the new analysts are "head-hunted" repeatedly by recruiters enticing them with more money. The average tenure of a security analyst is only 1-3 years with a single company.[6] Companies today offer very lucrative compensation packages tied to the amount of time spent with the company. A common practice is to use stock options spread out over 3-4 years to ensure the worker remains at the company.

Once a SOC analyst is proficient at their job and feels they are no longer challenged, it might be time for them to seek a higher position. One of the most common paths upward is to become a senior SOC analyst. The "senior" title comes with better pay and additional responsibilities such as mentoring the junior analysts that join the SOC. Senior SOC analysts also handle more complicated work as junior analysts will escalate challenging items to their seniors to resolve. Being in this position allows an analyst

---

[6]www.indeed.com/salaries/security-analyst-Salaries

to become more technical and gives them the opportunity to learn how to train and mentor others. This role is an excellent way to become a SOC manager, grooming them for their next leadership role in the SOC. Almost everywhere in the United States, the senior SOC analyst pays over six figures.

As a new SOC analyst, set stretch goals for yourself to reach this milestone. However, that leaves the hiring manager with your spot open again!

Another problem that SOC managers struggle with is burnout or alert fatigue. An example of this could be when analysts are watching so many alerts that something important is overlooked or "lost in the noise." SOC analysts usually work in shifts with 8-, 10-, or 12-hour days, sometimes evening and overnight shifts, and at some point, the task might seem brainless. It's not brainless work; in fact, most people will find SOC analyst work exhausting. It's easy to get complacent when the work becomes second nature and can get monotonous. Most everyone in a SOC is brilliant and constantly needs to be challenged.

The third challenge that SOC managers face is that the SOC is a 24/7/365 operation, which means they need coverage outside of regular business hours and on holidays. Many international companies utilize the "follow the sun" SOC model. That is when companies build three SOCs in different geographical locations for 24-hour coverage. Typically, companies will have a SOC in the United States, a second in Singapore or Australia, and the third in India or Europe. However, there are use cases where companies require analysts from a specific nationality to work with their data. It's especially true in staffing a Managed Security Services Provider (MSSP).

Hiring for early morning and overnight shifts is not an easy task, and the people that fill them don't stay for long before wanting to move to regular business hours. Tyler's first security job was working as a second-shift analyst in a SOC at an MSSP. He was in a position in life where it worked out well for him. He had a base salary and was offered a small shift differential on top of it for working the second shift. He was freshly out of college, and who needed to wake up before noon anyway? He credits his career to making that sacrifice because it gave him invaluable experience that still serves him today. He decided he had to take his experience and run after only a year. It was a hard decision because it was a great company, but he couldn't wait for a day shift to open up. The night hours started to take a toll. It is nobody's fault, but it is another challenge of the SOC revolving door.

SOCs aren't going away anytime soon. The demand for the SOC grows with every new privacy law, every new compliance and regulation that companies must adhere to. A SOC is an expensive cost center in business. Unless the SOC is part of your product that brings in revenue, it loses the company money. The more SOC analysts they need to hire, the more companies are looking for creative ways to reduce the money spent on a SOC. This demand has given birth to a set of tools promising to automate some of what a SOC analyst does on a day-to-day basis, but it presents challenges that the industry hasn't solved (yet).

Note   Security Orchestration Automation and Response (SOAR) tools promise to reduce the number of hours spent by SOC analysts to complete a task. This is explained in detail in Chapter 7.

What This Book Is About

As of late 2020, there are roughly three million cybersecurity professionals in the world, but that number must grow by more than double to meet the increasing demand. What does that mean for you? It means that individuals with the right skills and qualifications should find it relatively easy to land a job. If we look into the hiring challenges that companies face today, it becomes clear that technically proficient cybersecurity professionals continue to be in short supply, not to mention it is also difficult to find candidates with business acumen. Cybersecurity professionals are needed because the Internet is a global war zone. Anyone and everyone on the Internet is constantly being barraged by attacks every few seconds. Cybersecurity professionals protect enterprises from a successful intrusion and respond effectively when an attacker gets through the barricades. There are great opportunities out there for professionals, and because the demand is so high, people who are qualified and have the skills in this book will be hired.

A candidate not only has to be technically skilled but also needs to know how to interact with the other parts of the business in a way that shows they understand business goals, objectives, and culture. Recognizing these challenges faced by cybersecurity hiring managers allows you to prepare for your interview or have advancement discussions with your boss. This book will arm you with tools that you need to build a good strategy for transitioning onto the front lines of cybersecurity.

When you read this book, we will provide you with the knowledge needed to help you with the business acumen challenges by explaining how a typical security organization is structured from the top down. Understanding the "big picture" view of cybersecurity is imperative because, as mentioned, understanding how things work inside a company is fundamental to how effective you will become as a Security Operations Center (SOC) analyst.

At a basic level, similarly funded cybersecurity programs are usually equally structured, with the exception where security is the product of the business. Managed Security Services Providers (MSSP) sell security solutions to customers, and many of these SOC roles are customer-facing. MSSPs tend to have a more robust hierarchy and will sometimes include positions such as a SOC director. The culture is a bit different in our experience as well, security is how MSSPs make money, and the CEO is always the "security guy."

In-house SOCs, on the other hand, tend to be granted more control over the enterprise's security architecture and engineering. The SOC analysts can get "into the weeds" of the infrastructure and learn the ins and outs of the network. Where the customer of an MSSP is external, third-party companies and organizations, the customer of the in-house SOC is the company itself. These SOC analysts are given more power to intervene during security incidents to remediate the situation. Although this might sound like a good thing, one poor decision can negatively impact the entire network and become a "resume-generating event".

Once you're hired, the first day in the Security Operations Center can be the most overwhelming experience you will ever have. You might feel out of your league with all of the buzzwords, new security tools you've never heard of, and technologies that weren't exactly covered by formal education. To top it off, you're considered a cybersecurity expert by those not in the field, and people will be looking to you for advice. It can take up to a year to get settled in and feel comfortable enough to take a breath. Remember to give yourself some slack and be patient. We aim to help you shorten the time of discomfort. We will help you solve the technical proficiency challenges hiring managers struggle with by familiarizing you with the standard tools that you might use on a day-to-day basis.

We will help you with technical proficiency challenges by guiding you to think like a SOC analyst. There are many ways to learn how to think analytically, and for some people, it will come more naturally than others. It's important to know that it is not out of reach to anyone, and we mean anyone. Teaching hard technical skills is something better left to the professionals at SANS, but this book will fill in the gaps that you need to start your SOC analyst career quickly.

The demand for cybersecurity is enormous, but the unfilled jobs are a result of a lack of the right kind of applicants – not the number of them. Plenty of people want the salaries and lifestyles of the industry's practitioners. However, hiring managers need help now, and they will hire the candidate that requires the least amount of training. They need to hire someone that can do the job by yesterday!

Through the course of this book, we will help to identify the priorities and goals of the people and business units outside of the SOC that you will interact with daily so that you can thoughtfully approach them. We'll show you how to use language in your conclusions that protects you and your company while you are new to this role.

Summary

The need for cybersecurity professionals is growing at a rapid rate. Much faster than the industry can train candidates and fill positions. Hiring managers are faced with challenges that are at least twofold: they can't find technically proficient candidates, and they can't find candidates that know the business. This mix of hard and soft skills is incredibly important to have, but also increasingly important as your cybersecurity career progresses.

The cybersecurity analyst occupation is projected to grow 32% from 2018 to 2028 in the United States alone, compared with 12% growth for IT-related positions and only 5% total growth for all occupations. When the world is in crisis, cybersecurity workers are essential. The demand for the work that we do increases dramatically, but often this means the current workforce must work longer and harder. Hiring additional people can take many months.

The SOC analyst is the lowest barrier of entry into cybersecurity, and this book will help prepare you for landing your first role. The revolving-door challenge of a SOC means that there are always new positions opening up for you to apply for. In the next chapter, we will discuss what job titles to look for, typical job posting websites, and strategies on how to turn your job application into an interview.

CHAPTER 2

Areas of Expertise in Cybersecurity

In this chapter, we'll discuss the many disciplines that make up a successful company, their scope of duties, and how their role brings them into contact with the Security Operations Center (SOC). We'll also cover the external organizations that the SOC might interact within their day-to-day job.

Your time as a SOC analyst will bring you into contact with many teams from within your organization. Everyone, including the CEO, could be involved in a security investigation. However, the SOC plays an essential role in the functions of other teams as well, including external organizations. This chapter will break down the teams into three sections: information security teams, internal teams, and external teams. So, let's get started.

Information Security

Information security teams in most large organizations today are made up of three groups: **operations**, **engineering**, and **architecture**. The size of the companies' enterprise network is usually the main factor in determining if the team is staffed internally or outsourced to third-party organizations. Some mid-sized organizations might combine the duties of two teams to save costs. Regardless of who staffs these positions, the scope of responsibility for each group is different and distinct.

© Tyler Wall and Jarrett Rodrick 2021
T. Wall and J. Rodrick, *Jump-start Your SOC Analyst Career*,
https://doi.org/10.1007/978-1-4842-6904-6_2

11

Let's start with an easy one. The **Security Operations** team is where you work as a SOC analyst. I hope by now you've learned that "SOC" is an acronym for Security Operations Center. Right, now that we've gotten that knee-slapper out of the way, let's talk briefly about the Security Operations' scope of duties. As discussed in Chapter 1, Security Operations is home to the SOC, threat intelligence, digital forensics, and incident response. Each subgroup works together to ensure that day-to-day operations are running smoothly.

The **SOC** is responsible for monitoring, investigating, and remediating security events. Their scope of responsibility depends on who is staffing the SOC. As previously discussed, SOCs can be internal to the company or outsourced to an MSSP. Internal SOCs typically have higher privileges to take remedial actions during an incident, where Managed Security Services Providers (MSSPs) usually must report the incident to a customer's information technology (IT) team. The key benefit to an internal SOC vs. an MSSP is the ability of the internal SOC to learn the details of a single network. MSSPs have multiple customers and must monitor several enterprise networks at once. This leaves the SOC analysts at a disadvantage as they never truly learn the granular details of a customer's enterprise.

Threat intelligence (TI) is usually a smaller team that's focused on researching new threat reports, determining if the new threat is a danger to the company, and provides pertinent details to management and other information security teams. In some situations, the TI team is responsible for managing the Threat Intelligence Platform, which serves as a single point of collection for indicators of compromise and intelligence reports from multiple intel sources.

Some typical intel sources are threat feeds such as AlienVault or Talos Intelligence and Open Source Intelligence. The best threat feeds require a subscription and can get expensive. However, they have dedicated security researchers teamed with intelligence collection specialists to generate high fidelity reports. Open Source Intelligence, or OSINT for short, can provide excellent intel if you have a team dedicated to sifting through it all. A quick Google search for "Open Source Intel Feeds" will net you a plethora of top ten lists of the best OSINT feeds out there.

The **Digital Forensics and Incident Response (DFIR)** team is responsible for conducting investigations on long and enduring incidents. While the SOC does conduct the initial investigation, at some point the incident transitions to the DFIR team. Any engagements with legal, privacy, fraud, or external law enforcement organizations get filtered through the DFIR team, essentially becoming the subject matter experts on such matters. In most organizations, the DFIR team works hand in hand with threat intelligence to conduct threat hunting.

Definition   Threat hunting is an advanced security function that combines a proactive methodology, innovative technology, highly skilled people, and in-depth threat intelligence to find and stop the malicious, often hard-to-detect activities executed by stealth attackers that automated defenses may miss before they can execute on their objectives.[1]

The **Security Architecture** team is unique to large organizations and is focused on enforcing best security practices and compliance controls while implementing new technology in the enterprise. Let's look at an example: Your company wants to move its on-premises database into a cloud solution such as Amazon AWS or Microsoft Azure. It's the Security Architecture team's job to work with the database and cloud administrators to ensure that the systems and data being migrated into the cloud are as secure as possible. This team is usually composed of senior

---

[1]www.carbonblack.com/resources/definitions/what-is-cyber-threat-hunting/

security specialists with several years of experience in cybersecurity. Some organizations will outsource this to a third-party security consulting firm due to the limited scope of work needed for individual projects.

A common practice for Security Architecture teams is to have specialists who have concentrated their skills in a single field. To name a few, some of these fields are host-based security, network security, and virtualization or cloud security. Depending on the objectives of the company, security architects will devise the security and logging plan for the project to ensure a proper balance of security and cost-saving. Security Architecture is one of the many pathways for a SOC analyst to move up in their career. You should have at least 4-5 years of cybersecurity experience before considering a move into Security Architecture.

Finally, the **Security Engineering** team is responsible for deploying, managing, and maintaining the enterprise's security tools and appliances. Many smaller companies will combine this function with the SOC analysts. They're able to do this due to the small footprint of the network; however, large companies will staff this team internally. Whether this role is staffed or handled by the SOC, security engineers are also responsible for updating and tuning the security tools.

Many organizations will assign a single technology group to an engineer. For example, an engineer might be responsible for maintaining the network intrusion detection systems (NIDS) deployed on the network. It's essential to understand the need for cross-leveling of skills here. A single person managing the NIDS would leave the organization in a predicament if the employee were to tender their notice. A best practice is to have a minimum of two engineers on a technology group; this allows for a checks-and-balances approach that limits the risk of a single point of failure.

The number one customer of the Security Engineering team is the SOC. Because these teams work so closely together, security engineer is a natural progression for SOC analysts in the ladder upward. This role requires advanced knowledge of how to administer systems and technologies. If your SOC relies on a Security Engineering team, and you wish to sharpen your engineering skills, take on some projects in your spare time at home. Learn a new technology group, such as virtualization or containers. The best way to learn this job is by doing it. So get out there and experiment, and when you fail, delete it all and start again.

To wrap it up, the **Vulnerability Management** team is responsible for identifying, cataloging, and remediating new and existing vulnerabilities throughout the enterprise network. Periodically, vulnerability scanners such as Nessus, OpenVAS, and BurpSuite scan important infrastructure to compare system baselines for changes to their configurations. Many companies staff in-house "Red Teams" to conduct cyclic penetration tests on the network. Otherwise, penetration testing is outsourced to a consulting company.

In summary, most organizations have some embodiment of these four teams: Security Operations, Security Architecture, Security Engineering, and Vulnerability Management. Whether the team is outsourced or owned by the SOC, the roles exist in every company. Each is a puzzle piece that fits together to form a well-rounded cybersecurity program. No one is more important than the other, and I ask that you remember this as you move forward in your career. On that note, let's move on to the next section.

Internal Teams

As you gain and demonstrate experience as a SOC analyst, opportunities to interact with teams outside of the SOC will occur. These opportunities are an excellent way to stand out and make a great impression on your leadership. Regardless of the task, you should approach each encounter with external teams with a high level of professionalism and confidence. You'll find that when you've put in maximum effort toward the task, word of your accomplishments will make it back to your supervisor.

And of course, the reverse is true as well. The last thing you want is for your supervisor to learn that you failed to contribute to a task. They tend to remember those conversations when reviewing compensation adjustments.

Let's first talk about **Management**. Technically, not all of management works outside the SOC. The SOC has a manager, and usually, somewhere up the chain, there's a director. But, management makes business decisions, so this topic will cover the standard positions and scope of responsibility of those in management. It's important to know that every organization is different in how they staff their management team. We'll start in the SOC with the SOC manager and work upward to the executive staff.

The **SOC manager** is the direct and first-line supervisor for all SOC analysts. Your interactions with them begin in the interview process as they're also responsible as the hiring manager for the open analyst positions. SOC managers have a wide range of duties, everything from mentoring the junior analysts to managing the image of the SOC to other teams. In fact, the SOC manager has so many duties that there could be an entire chapter dedicated to the topic. We'll begin with their responsibilities to you, the newly hired SOC analyst.

The SOC manager is responsible for all aspects of compensation for the analysts under them, including the offer letter when you first applied, bonus payouts, and promotions. However, promotions can't happen without mentorship, and that's also a large part of their duties. Each company has different mentorship requirements, but you can expect to sit down with your manager and discuss personal and business goals. Your progress toward achieving these goals is taken into account during the bonus and promotion decisions. Time-off requests, work schedules, and SOC duty assignments are all decided upon by the SOC manager.

The SOC manager is also responsible for generating reports on the number and type of security events the SOC sees to upper management. These reports inform the members of the executive staff on the latest trends of cyberattacks that are targeting the company. The SOC manager is the first level of the management team and is by far one of the hardest jobs in information security. In a later chapter, we will cover the SOC manager more in depth. For now, let's move on.

The **SOC director** is the next step up in the chain of managers to the SOC. This title is different for almost every company; some examples are "Director of Security Operations," "Director of Threat Management," and "Director of IT Security." Regardless of title, this position is usually the SOC manager's supervisor. They're responsible for the overall strategic decisions that face the company regarding cybersecurity, including budgeting requests, SOC staffing approval, and reporting to executive leadership. They also coordinate with other directors to plan and coordinate joint projects. We'll cover them more later.

The next rung in the management ladder is the **Chief Information Security Officer** or CISO for short. Depending on the company, the responsibilities of the CISO range considerably. Due to this, we won't spend too much time discussing the CISO. All you need to understand from a SOC analyst perspective is the CISO is responsible for the high-level decisions regarding information security. They will most likely be the first executive officer you'll meet, and depending on your company, the CISO likely reports directly to the CEO. So, no pressure trying to make an excellent first impression.

That'll wrap it up for the management team; from here let's move on to some of the common organizations you'll work with as a SOC analyst. Each team we discuss will have a similar management structure as the SOC. I'll skip going into detail about the team members and focus on the scope of the team itself.

The **Risk Management** team is responsible for measuring, reporting, and mitigating the company's risk levels. In regard to cybersecurity, they'll look at the likelihood of a compromise, determine the impact on the business if the attack happened, and generate a report to management on the risk. This data allows management to make an informed decision to

17

assume or mitigate the risk. Most likely, if all this sounds familiar, you've learned about risk matrices somewhere along the way

"But how does the SOC assist the Risk Management Team?" I'm so glad you asked. Risk Management teams are not cybersecurity experts. Their understanding of attacks and compromises is severely limited to what they read in the news. That's when the SOC consults to define the impact of a compromise. An example of a SOC consultation would be to describe how a critical system is vulnerable to a particular type of compromise. Maybe you're asked what security control would best stop the attack before it happens. Regardless of the request from Risk Management, the goal is to provide them with the worst-case scenario. To measure risk, Risk Management needs to know the most dangerous outcome for the company and how often it might occur.

The **Governance and Compliance** team ensures "the overall management approach board members and senior executives use to control and direct an organization"[2] is disseminated and adhered. They also ensure the company meets or exceeds compliance standards related to certain industries. An example of this would be the Payment Card Industry Data Security Standard (PCI DSS), which enforces controls around payment and card systems. The purpose of compliance is to ensure that proper cybersecurity practices are followed in a uniform manner. There are several global compliance standards, and each has a different set of controls, although some overlap. Table 2-1 lists the common and well-known compliance standards.

---

[2]https://insights.diligent.com/entity-governance/the-correlation-between-corporate-governance-and-compliance

Table 2-1. *Common Compliance Standards*

Payment Card Industry Data Security Standard (PCI DSS)	`www.pcisecuritystandards.org/`
International Organization for Standardization (ISO 27001)	`www.iso.org/`
Cybersecurity Maturity Model Certification (CMMC)	`www.acq.osd.mil/cmmc/`
Health Insurance Portability and Accountability Act of 1996 (HIPAA) Security Rule	`www.hhs.gov/hipaa/for-professionals/security/`
Information Security Registered Assessors Program (IRAP)	`www.cyber.gov.au/irap/`
System and Organization Controls (SOC)	`www.aicpa.org/interestareas/frc/`

The most common interaction the SOC will have with Governance and Compliance teams is during the auditing process. The SOC plays a vital role in providing evidence of compliance for the Audit team. Some common evidence requests might be logs collected, process documentation, and a security event walk-through. We'll cover more about the Audit team later in this chapter.

Definition   Auditing is the information gathering and analysis of assets to ensure such things as policy compliance and security from vulnerabilities.[3]

---

[3]`www.sans.org/security-resources/glossary-of-terms/`

The next team we'll cover is the **Privacy and Legal** team. Usually, you'll interact with Privacy and Legal during security incidents that involve evidence collection or public disclosure of a compromise. In the previous chapter, we briefly discussed the Capital One data breach.[4] The privacy half of this team was responsible for identifying the nature of the data that was stolen. Working with legal, together they inform executive leadership on disclosure requirements, legal obligations, and options to pursue actions against the attacker. In the case of Capital One, the Privacy and Legal team notified victims of the data breach and assisted the FBI in apprehending the suspect.

Let's segue to our final team for this section, the **Fraud** team. The Fraud team works hand in hand with Privacy and Legal in investigations of a data breach to determine if the data has been leaked, sold, or used for malicious means. For example, the data stolen from Capital One included 140,000 US Social Security Numbers. The Fraud team is responsible for investigations tied to the use of stolen data such as identity theft or data brokerage on the dark web. The Fraud team's responsibilities shift depending on the company's industry. A software company's Fraud team might scour the Internet for license key generators, while a manufacturing company has their Fraud team looking for signs of stolen blueprints.

External Teams

For this chapter, external teams are defined as any team that does not work for your company. So far, we've covered information security and internal teams that the SOC will interact with to accomplish business objectives. Your interaction with external teams requires special considerations. The most important note is that you are a representative of your organization and company. You must consider how you interact with and what is said

---

[4]www.capitalone.com/facts2019/

to external organizations, as it might unintentionally affect the business. If you stay professional and use tact, you will succeed!

The first external team we'll discuss is **government** agencies, and they'll play a critical role in any country. Whether it's for compliance, reports of data breaches, or interpreting privacy laws, the SOC will eventually find itself interacting with the local or federal government. As both authors are located in the United States, we'll cover what we know and not speculate on other country's stance on cybersecurity. I urge you to research local laws and regulations in your region to prepare yourself when interacting with your local government agency.

There are different types of government agencies that we need to cover, and the SOC will interact with each one in various capacities. **Law enforcement** agencies will be the most common government entity you'll encounter. Some examples of law enforcement agencies in the United States are the Federal Bureau of Investigation (FBI), Department of Homeland Security (DHS), and State and Local Police. Like the Legal and Privacy team, the SOC will most likely work to provide evidence of data breaches or insider threats to the investigating agency. When communicating with law enforcement agencies, it's important to only state facts. Try to remain professional and pay respect to the members of the agency you are working beside. The majority of individuals you'll deal with won't be cybersecurity analysts, so speak in common terms.

The second government entity we'll discuss is **military and intelligence agencies.** Today, many companies provide services or goods to their federal government, and most countries have cybersecurity regulations that must be followed by companies that do business with the government. This comes in the form of tighter compliance controls and mandatory reporting requirements. A benefit of working with the government is the shared threat intelligence provided by the network of companies that work with the government. In the United States, companies that work with the federal government can join the Defense Industrial Base Cybersecurity (DIB CS) program. This program allows companies to share threat reports, indicators of compromise, and malware samples in a central location. The Department of Defense (DoD) also provides threat reports and alerts based on intelligence collected by military or intelligence agencies.

The last government organization we'll cover is **regulatory agencies.** Regulatory agencies are bodies created by a legislature act to set a baseline of standards for a particular field of activity in the private sector of the economy and then enforces those standards. Regulatory agencies are commonly broken out into business sectors; for example, the US Department of Health and Human Services regulates the HIPAA compliance standards.

Not all regulatory bodies are government-affiliated; the International Organization for Standardization is an independent, nongovernmental international organization with a membership of 164 national standards bodies. Since nongovernment regulatory agencies can't enforce compliance or issue punishment to companies out of compliance, government agencies who adopt compliance standards such as ISO 27001 will assume responsibility for enforcement and punishment. In this model, a committee of representatives from the member countries developed new and revamped compliance standards.

The second external team we'll discuss is **Auditor** teams. Auditors play a significant role in a company's path to regulatory compliance and will be a source of many headaches for the SOC. The auditor's primary responsibility is to understand the compliance standards and the security controls that satisfy the requirement. Next, they apply their knowledge and expertise in their field to compare a company's security posture against the compliance standards. Let's look at an example of how an auditor might interact with the SOC during a compliance engagement by looking at a PCI DSS Version 1.2 controls[5] in Table 2-2.

---

[5]https://www.pcisecuritystandards.org/pdfs/pci_ssc_quick_guide.pdf

Table 2-2. *Excerpt from PCI CSS Quick Guide*

Goals	PCI DSS Requirements
Build and Maintain a Secure Network	1. Install and maintain a firewall configuration to protect cardholder data 2. Do not use vendor-supplied defaults for system passwords and other security parameters
Protect Cardholder Data	3. Protect stored cardholder data 4. Encrypt transmission of cardholder data across open, public networks
Maintain a Vulnerability Management Program	5. Use and regularly update antivirus software or programs 6. Develop and maintain secure systems and applications
Implement Strong Access Control Measures	7. Restrict access to cardholder data by business need-to-know 8. Assign a unique ID to each person with computer access 9. Restrict physical access to cardholder data
Regularly Monitor and Test Networks	10. Track and monitor all access to network resources and cardholder data 11. Regularly test security systems and processes
Maintain an Information Security Policy	12. Maintain a policy that addresses information security for employees and contractors

The goal, "Regularly Monitor and Test Networks," is a typical example of data the SOC will be responsible for providing. Specifically, the SOC would be the team monitoring access to network resources, and the data auditors will ask to see will most likely be in the SOC's SIEM. Each auditor is different, so the exact data they'll ask for will vary depending on the experience level and individual preference. Some auditors will request for the SOC to give a live demo of their ability to access and monitor the data, while others will request screenshots of the monitoring platform and the data held within. Depending on the compliance standard, audits will happen anywhere from every 3 months to annually. Also, depending on your company, the SOC might be responsible for providing evidence to multiple audit teams throughout the year.

As a new SOC analyst, you won't likely interact with the auditors directly. If a demo is requested, it's usually handled by a senior analyst due to their experience with the company's data sources and monitoring portfolio. Your manager and team lead will own the responsibility of planning and coordinating with the compliance and audit teams, and your tasks begin with evidence collection.

Let's move on to our final team for this chapter, and likely the most common external team you'll interact with as a junior analyst. **Vendors** are external product or service providers that have sold a product to your company or are attempting to sell a product. Any tool the SOC uses, which wasn't created by your company, came from a vendor. The SOC's interaction level with existing vendors will be limited to requesting assistance with issues, feature requests, and bug reports. However, you might be asked to join a tool demo or proof of concept (POC) evaluation of a security tool. Working with vendors can be a great networking opportunity; leaving a good impression with the vendor could lead to future job offers if you decide to move away from the SOC.

When working with existing vendors, there are specific ethical concerns around requesting features or accepting gifts. It's important to remember that you're a representative of your company. Vendors who provide an existing service or product could take your feature request and bill your company for the hours spent on the work. That shouldn't deter you from asking for new features. When communicating with the vendor, be sure to ask them if the company will be billed before any agreement is made.

Similarly, when communicating with vendors trying to sell your company a product or service, it's important not to promise anything to the vendor. The best conversation you can have with a vendor providing a demo or POC is by offering your honest feedback on their product. Good or bad, they will take your feedback to their company for product changes. So when providing your thoughts on their product, be sure to offer constructive criticism. Comments like "your product adds no value for us" and "we could build this ourselves" is a surefire way to get you removed from future vendor conversations.

Summary

Working in the SOC brings you into contact with many other teams, both from within and external to your company. Each team covered in this chapter combines to shape your SOC's daily scope of duties. The team names and roles discussed in this chapter are not standardized from company to company. As previously mentioned, some team member responsibilities might belong to the SOC. Regardless of whether the positions exist, the team's functions are required for a company to succeed in the cyberspace domain.

We've talked previously about our purpose for this book and how we hope to prepare you for a great, new career in cybersecurity by way of the SOC. Consider the overhead of having to teach a new SOC analyst the functions of each team member, external organization, and government entity for a moment. This chapter helps you set yourself up for success by providing a cursory introduction to the areas of expertise in cybersecurity. Whether you're working with your local law enforcement to investigate a malicious insider or collecting audit evidence to the compliance team, your better understanding of the groups and their roles and responsibilities will help to make you stand out as a productive member of the SOC team.

CHAPTER 3

Job Hunting

This chapter will cover the strategies on how to find a SOC analyst job including common job titles, what job boards to use, resume tips, networking with other professionals, and common interview questions.

If you find yourself at the crossroads of your old life and finding a new career in cybersecurity, then this chapter will give you tips and tools to find a job in the cybersecurity industry. This might mean that you are graduating from college and looking to start your career, or this might mean that you have been in IT for a while and you are looking to dive into cybersecurity, or maybe it means you are an honored vet looking to transition into the civilian space. Whatever the case may be, there are a few things you should know.

Networking

Word of mouth is your friend! It is important to grow your network. Having a broad network of people that you can talk to professionally not only opens you up to new opportunities but gives you people to discuss your new ideas with. Professional connections help you stay on top of the latest trends such as news or technical techniques that will benefit you greatly.

© Tyler Wall and Jarrett Rodrick 2021
T. Wall and J. Rodrick, *Jump-start Your SOC Analyst Career*,
https://doi.org/10.1007/978-1-4842-6904-6_3

There are many opportunities to get involved in projects or communities local to your area. Some of these include:

- **2600:** 2600 (2600.org) is an organization that has deep roots in the hacker culture. Today, it exists as a website, meetup space, conference, and magazine to name a few. The history of hacking is fascinating, and their name comes from 2600hz, which is the frequency at which a plastic whistle found inside a Captain Crunch box sounded when you blew it. Blown into a payphone and it allowed the hacker to make free phone calls.

- **Defcon:** The diamond jewel of hacking conferences. The defcon conference is traditionally held annually in the summer in Las Vegas, NV, and is considered a pilgrimage for anyone in infosec! There is so much to do, so many knobs to twist, bells to ding, and big red buttons to push you will never have time to do it all. What makes this conference great for your career is that recruiters love it! I have heard so many stories of people getting job offers on the spot at defcon. Defcon is even better if you volunteer at the events. You will meet more people and at a deeper level. Additionally, defcon has "defcon groups" which are smaller defcon meetings in your local areas usually on a monthly basis. This is also a great way to network with your local infosec peers to see what is going on in your local infosec industry and hopefully pick up a lead!

- **BSides:** BSides is a popular conference that is held locally in a lot of cities and also during the same time frame as defcon in Las Vegas. It is fairly popular and offers a lot of value. Tickets are usually pretty cheap (and free if you volunteer), and it gives you access to what is going on and the people in your area.

- **OWASP:** Open Web Application Security Project (OWASP) is a nonprofit foundation that works to improve the security of software. Through community-led open source software projects, hundreds of local chapters worldwide, tens of thousands of members, and leading educational and training conferences, the OWASP Foundation is the source for developers and technologists to secure the Web.

- **Hackerspaces and Makerspaces:** These meetups in your local areas are a great way to meet people, tinker, pull knobs, and push buttons. Sometimes these meetings will allow their members to give presentations in a show and tell format, and that is a great way to build your presentation skills.

If you have been attending meetings in your surrounding areas, don't forget to take a pencil and notepad with you to write down emails and contact info of the people you meet. It is not weird and doesn't feel uncomfortable, everyone there is there for the same reason, and you'd be the lucky one with a notepad. Most people would feel flattered you'd care enough to write their information on the notepad. Tell your new friends you want to keep in contact and be on the lookout for them. Follow up with everyone the day after, and send them your resume to share with others.

Once you have attended a few meetings, you can start to build a network of like-minded community members to associate with. Once you have started to build your network, you might have a few leads, but you also want to not have all your eggs in one basket. You will want to apply for jobs on traditional job posting boards.

Applying for Jobs

We would like to explain to you how to perform a job hunt. First off, you need to get your resume together. It takes a lot of trial and error to perfect a resume, but you can also have a professional help you build a good one. A resume can take form in many styles, but it will have the same basic information:

- **Contact Information:** At the top of your resume should include your full name, email, phone number, address, and LinkedIn.

- **Summary:** A high-level summary of your skills and qualifications as it pertains to the position you are applying for should be included so the reader can quickly identify your strengths to see if you are a good fit for the role.

- **Education:** List any formal education and certifications you might have. Include degrees that may not necessarily be technology related if you have it, but do not include certifications that do not pertain to the role you are applying for.

- **Skills:** List your skills that relate to the position you are applying for.

- **Job Experience:** List your previous job-related experience. Some resume writers will strategically list your experience in a way that best targets the role you are looking to fill, and would tell you to only go back 5 years or two pages, whichever comes first.

An optional section for "**Objective**" may be used if you are performing a lateral move or career change to explain your intent for changing careers. Keep your resume to under three pages to prevent overskimming by the readers. The benefit of having a professional resume writing service is they will share a document with you and probe you with questions until they get all of the information out of you about your previous experience and then write it in a way that is quickly and easily consumed.

Once your resume is together, you can move forward to a job search. There are several job posting websites that have proven successful for us; however, I have had the most success with LinkedIn. When we are searching for a job, I usually purchase their premium membership so that I am able to see the statistics for each job I am applying for, send InMail messages to hiring managers or recruiters for a company I am interested in, and see who is looking at my profile. Also, Google has a good aggregation of jobs to search through. Using Google, you are able to set up and configure job alerts specifically for cybersecurity jobs.

The security analyst position is the job that you will be able to land the easiest as a first step into information security. There is a revolving door in most SOCs, and the position for security analyst opens frequently. The three titles that you want to look for first are:

- Security analyst

- Information security analyst

- Security Operations Center (SOC) analyst

Note   While the SOC analyst might be the lowest paying of the three job titles, we believe that since the trajectory of salaries is so steep, in the long run it would be best to even take a mild pay cut just to get your foot in the door with security. Senior security analysts make well into the six-figure ranges in most companies, and that is just one step up.

If you are mobile and can move anywhere, your odds for finding a good fit quickly are pretty good. If you live far outside of a big city, then your options may be more limited. Most SOCs require you to be on-site for security purposes, but that seems to be changing post COVID-19. You may be able to find a remote SOC analyst position, but you may have more options in your nearest big city.

Common Interview Questions

The following is a list of common interview questions that might be asked during an interview for a junior SOC analyst. Some are very basic and some are harder, but we feel if you can answer these questions you have the required knowledge to become a SOC analyst:

1. What is an RFC 1918 address?

   a. Do you know them?

2. Define a Class A, B, or C network.

3. What are the seven phases of the cyber kill chain?

4. What is the purpose of the Mitre ATT&CK Framework?

5. What is the difference between TCP and UDP?

6. What are ports 80, 443, 22, 23, 25, and 53?

7. What is data exfiltration?

   a. What Windows protocol is commonly used for data exfiltration?

8. Do you have a home lab?

   a. Explain it.

9. What is AWS?

   a. Explain how you've used it.

10. What is a DMZ, and why is it a common target for cyberattacks?

The importance of having technical knowledge cannot be overstated. The above questions are pretty simple, but you might be surprised to learn that seven out of ten candidates don't know the common TCP/UDP ports used by modern services like SMB, NTP, and SSH. I highly suggest using a common study guide to prepare for your interview. An example of this is the website *Quizlet.com.* They provide a flashcard style learning platform for information technology certifications like Network+ or Security+. Both of these certification's flashcard decks can help brush up your knowledge before an interview.

Despite the need for a basic understanding of information technology, that only covers half of the requirement to be a SOC analyst. An analyst should be a critical thinker and possess an acumen for problem solving. Interviewers will usually test a candidate's ability for problem solving with scenario-based questions. Let's cover some scenarios I've seen and used to conduct interviews:

1. "You are a tier 1 SOC analyst, responsible for monitoring the SOC inbox for user-reported incidents. The SOC receives an email from the VP of Human Resources stating that they can't access their personal cloud drive. The VP knows this against company policy, but the VP is adamant that this is required for legitimate business requirements."

   a. Do you process the access request for the VP?

   b. What is your response to the VP?

   c. Who else should you include in the reply email?

2. "You are monitoring the SIEM dashboard for new security events. A network IDS alert is triggered, and you begin investigating. You see a large amount of network traffic over UDP port 161 originating from dozens of internal IP addresses, all with the same, internal destination IP address. Some quick Googling shows that UDP port 161 is used for by the Simple Network Management Protocol and the byte count of the traffic is miniscule."

    a. Do you think this is data exfiltration?

    b. If this is not data exfiltration, what legitimate services could cause this alert?

    c. What team could provide an explanation for the traffic?

The first scenario is an example of what you might be asked when applying for an entry level analyst role, while the second is a little more advanced. Let's go over what the interviewer is looking for.

Scenario 1 is designed to identify if the applicant can be easily intimidated by senior leadership in your organization. Information security is the responsibility of all members of the organization; it should not be waived for the convenience of one senior leader. The larger lesson here is about making risk-based decisions. A junior analyst should never assume the risk of policy exceptions.

The interviewer will ask how the applicant will respond to the VP as it will showcase their experience with customer service. Customer service is another very important task of a SOC analyst. Whether working for an MSSP or for a company internal SOC, there will be times when interfacing with other teams will require the analyst to show a certain level of tact and professionalism. The third question helps the interviewer to understand the prioritization skills of the analyst. If an analyst is working with a VP, there is a high probability there is a procedure around communicating with senior leadership within the org.

Scenario 2 is designed to test the applicant's critical thinking and technical knowledge while also providing the interviewer with insight to the applicant's investigative reasoning. This scenario also gives insight to the most important quality of a SOC analyst; if you don't know the answer, admit it. **The last thing the SOC team needs is a "know-it-all"; they are dangerous and toxic to the workplace.** If this book teaches you one thing, let it be this lesson. There will be questions you can't answer, and that's fine. The worst thing you can do is give a wrong answer with the confidence that you are 100% correct.

Remember that the above scenarios are examples only; each interviewer will use their own set of questions. The goal remains the same, to locate and select the best applicant for the position. Our goal is to assist you in becoming that applicant. The following are a few tricks and tips to help you become that "best applicant" for the position:

- Make the best first impression that you can.

    - Dress like a professional. Once the interview is scheduled, one of the first questions should be "what is the expected dress code for the interview?". Once you have this info, dress one level higher. For example, if you're told it will be business casual, add a sport coat or vest.

    - Bring printed copies of your resume, and offer a copy to the interviewer.

    - Be organized. This doesn't mean you need a briefcase, but consider a daily planner with pen and paper for note-taking.

- Use active listening techniques during the interview.

    - Keep eye contact with the interviewer.

    - Allow the interviewer to finish talking before answering.

- Maintain positive body language.

- Don't be afraid to ask for the interviewer to clarify or repeat their question.

- Have questions prepared for the interviewer about the role, the company, and professional growth.

  - "Will there be potential for this role to cross-train with other teams?"

  - "Does the company participate or support employees volunteering in local STEM programs?"

  - "What does the roadmap for progression look like for this role?"

- At the end of the interview, ask for feedback.

  - "In order to improve my interviewing skills, can you provide any positive or negative feedback?" This shows the interviewer that you care about self-growth and also provides you with the interviewer's thoughts on how the interview went.

Summary

The most important thing we want you to take out of this chapter is that you have tools to help you find a job. Use job boards, network with others in your area, and study to understand the answers to the common interview questions. The job market is growing fast, but in the future, the skills for analysts will change as SOC automation begins to mature. The resources that I've explained will be even more valuable to you as you move forward in time.

CHAPTER 4

Prerequisite Skills

This chapter will describe the prerequisite skills that you will need to land your first job in information security. We will also describe common backgrounds that pivot into the SOC analyst role well.

Knowing which topics you need to know to land your first role in infosec is crucial. While we can't teach you everything you need to know, this book will cover the fundamentals of security based upon a common baseline of knowledge. The common baseline of knowledge rests on network and security fundamentals. Most of the prerequisite knowledge can be gained by formal security certifications such as CompTIA Network+ and Security+. This chapter will discuss the concepts that you should have before interviewing. Let's talk about networking first.

Networking

Our first requisite skill we'll talk about is networking. No, this won't be about how to talk to people, but we will cover the basics of the modern TCP/IP stack. The Transmission Control Protocol and Internet Protocol were invented in the 1970s by DARPA scientists Vinton Cerf and Bob Kahn. At that time, there was not a standardized network standard. After over a decade of tests and refinement, the TCP/IP stack was officially launched in 1983 and was quickly adopted by the US Department of Defense. The DoD's adoption of the new protocol secured the TCP/IP's place as the standard moving forward.

© Tyler Wall and Jarrett Rodrick 2021
T. Wall and J. Rodrick, *Jump-start Your SOC Analyst Career*,
https://doi.org/10.1007/978-1-4842-6904-6_4

So what is the TCP/IP stack? Basically it can be viewed as a set of layers; each layer solves a set of problems around the transmission of data. The TCP/IP stack contains four layers. Alternatively, there is a seven-layer model called the Open Systems Interconnection (OSI) model. Today, the OSI model is more generally used as it provides a more granular view of the encapsulation process. For the purpose of continuity, we will use the OSI model going forward. Refer to Table 4-1 for TCP/IP and OSI model comparison.

Table 4-1. *TCP/IP and OSI Models*

TCP/IP Model	OSI Model
Layer 4 Application	Layer 7 – Application
	Layer 6 – Presentation
	Layer 5 – Session
Layer 3 Transport	Layer 4 – Transport
Layer 2 Network	Layer 3 – Network
Layer 1 Network Interface	Layer 2 – Data Link
	Layer 1 – Physical

Data encapsulation is the process of taking data from one layer of the OSI model and translating it into the next layer. A broad example is the process of turning the binary 1's and 0's in the physical layer into something that is human readable in the application layer. Regardless if you're viewing a web page or watching a video, data encapsulation is pivotal to the flow of data on our networks.

Note   An entire chapter could be dedicated to this topic; however, we suggest you search YouTube for "OSI Model Encapsulation." There are some great videos that break down the process with animations we can't properly depict here.

On the Internet today, there are two different kinds of IP addresses, IPv4 addresses and IPv6 addresses. IPv4 address space (e.g., 10.0.0.1) is what most people are familiar with, but due to changes in the Internet landscape, most especially the addition of the Internet of things, we are running out of available 32-bit IPv4 addresses. As a solution, the world has begun to use IPv6 devices (e.g., 2004:0cb8:82a3:08d3:1319:8a2e:0370:7334) which is a 64-bit solution. It is just mostly important to know that they are different, they look different, and we have run out new IPv4 addresses to issue people.

Another important thing to know about IP addresses is the difference between public network space and private network space. If you were to ping Google, the message exits my private network and traverses the public Internet until it hits the computer on the public Internet owned by Google, and then Google decides what to do with that message internally. Think of it like driving down through a modern neighborhood where the houses are right next to each other. As you drive, you can look to your left and right and see the front doors. You can walk up anyone's driveway and knock on their front door. Consider this: public address space of the Internet and private Internet address spaces are all the hallways and doors inside of the house after you enter the front door. Imagine a house has three types of areas: bedrooms, bathrooms, and common areas. In the scheme of the Internet, these three private home spaces are governed by something called the RFC1918 address space (Table 4-2). There are three IP address subnets in RFC1918. You can use any of them for any purpose; you're a homeowner and it's your house!

Table 4-2. RFC1918 Address Space

Address Space	Subnet Mask	Total IP Addresses
10.0.0.0–10.255.255.255	10.0.0.0/8	16,777,216
192.168.0.0–192.168.255.255	192.168.0.0/16	1,048,576
172.16.0.0–172.31.255.255	172.16.0.0/12	65,536

Due to the large number of hosts, in a corporate environment, it is most common to see the 10.0.0.0/8 address space used frequently.

It will be helpful to know the various common port numbers and the difference between TCP and UDP. TCP relies on an established connection called a three-way handshake and the UDP protocol. Think of UDP as the "Unreliable Dang Protocol" because the UDP protocol just sends messages and doesn't care if they get them there or not, whereas in the TCP connection if a piece of data is missed in transit, it will resend the missed packet and then put them back together in order. UDP services are mainly used for things such as video streaming where a glitch in the movie because of dropped packets wouldn't matter a lot. TCP connections are used when every bit of data needs to arrive at the destination, such as in a file transfer. If you are transferring a file, if all bits and bytes do not get to the destination, the file will not be able to be run.

Table 4-3 shows a cheatsheet table for port numbers.

Table 4-3. *Protocol Quick Reference*

Port Number	Protocol	Application
20	TCP	FTP Data
21	TCP	FTP Control
22	TCP	SSH
23	TCP	Telnet
25	TCP	SMTP
53	UDP, TCP	DNS
67,68	UDP	DHCP
69	UDP	TFTP
80	TCP	HTTP
110	TCP	POP3
161	UDP	SNMP
443	TCP	SSL

Next is the TCP three-way handshake process. This is important because this three-way handshake process establishes a connection between two hosts for a TCP connection. See Figure 4-1.

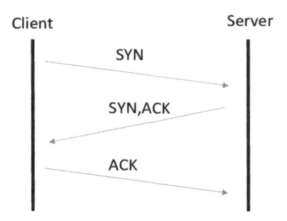

Figure 4-1. *TCP Three-Way Handshake*

To explain, let's say you are uploading a file to an image hosting website. Before the file transfer takes place, your computer would establish the connection to the server by sending an SYN packet. Then the server would send a SYN and Acknowledge packet back, and then your client will finally send the Acknowledge packet back, and the three-way handshake has completed.

How this translates into your new job is if a host on the public Internet is attacking the perimeter of the corporate network, you might only see a SYN packet. Most firewalls will drop this traffic if it isn't approved traffic and it isn't a big deal. However, if you are looking at a computer on your network that is under suspicion of communicating with a malicious host and they have completed the handshake process, there is a good chance they have actively communicated and data at some scale has been transferred.

Network Security

The basic tenets of security revolved around the concept of CIA Triad, not the Central Intelligence Agency but confidentiality, integrity, and availability. All of security can be broken down from these three high-level categories. Confidentiality is the secrecy of the information, making sure that the information can only be seen by the intended people, no more no less. Integrity revolves around the correctness of the data, making sure that the information you are consuming is the data that you intend to consume, complete and unaltered. Availability consists of making sure that the data is able to be used when it is needed to be used. For instance, a denial of service attack can make a website unavailable to people who try to visit it. This is an attack on availability.

Firewalls are superb for making sure that access to network resources are only available to those that need access. By use of access control lists (ACLs), firewalls can prevent the general Internet from accessing private network access. ACLs are an example of a confidentiality control as well as an availability control.

As stated earlier in this chapter, there is a delineation of public Internet space and RFC1918 private Internet space. This boundary is created by using networking appliances and is called the perimeter of a network. If you think of your network as a circle and everything inside of the circle is your private computers and resources and everything on the outside is the Internet, then the perimeter is the circle itself.

Also when thinking about access control models, the concept of least privilege should be considered. Least privilege simply is the concept that no one should have more access to information than is minimum. For instance, a janitor needs access to all areas in a building, but probably shouldn't require the same level of access to digital records.

While considering the principle of least privilege, separation of duties is also important. Separation of duties is the concept that important duties should be separated to provide less opportunity for fraud. The famous example to explain separation of duties is to separate the employee who balances the checkbooks from writing the checks. If they cooked the books (modified it to their advantage), they could easily write a check to themselves for the differences, and no one would ever know.

Cryptography

There are a few cryptography principles that you will need to know as well. The first is the difference between encryption vs. hashing. Basically, encrypting is changing the data in a way that makes it unreadable, but it is intended to be changed back in a way to make the message readable again.

Note   Takeaways to research on your own from encryption principles are knowing what public keys and private keys are and when they are used. Also, know what makes that key process different than using the same key to encrypt and decrypt.

Hashing is the process of taking a set of data and creating a unique fingerprint out of it. For instance, if you had a thousand lines of code, you could save it to a file and hash that file to a 128-bit MD5 hash that would look something similar to this:

97fbca75e134639d48bd83270ae9e045

The main difference between a hash and an encryption is that a hash is one way. There is not any viable way to turn the string above back into the characters "Cyber NOW Education Rulez."

Endpoint Security

According to Verizon's 2020 Data Breach Investigations Report[1], 90% of all malware infections come from emails. While talking about networking and network security is important. The front lines of the cybersecurity war are on your network endpoints. User laptops, smart phones, and printers are only a few of the targeted devices that attackers can compromise. The difficulty with endpoint security is the plethora of devices on the market. The majority of all devices run on one of these three operating system (OS) families: Windows, Unix, and MacOS.

Note   The Verizon Data Breach Report is perhaps the most respected publication in the cybersecurity industry. We would suggest taking a minute to review the latest breach report online to bring you up to speed with the industry's latest cyber statistics. This is a great topic during interviews!

When considering endpoint security, I've found the most valuable skill is the knowledge of how each one could be compromised or exploited. The following sections will cover the major operating systems and some of their common vulnerabilities.

Windows

Let's talk about Windows first as they are the global market leader for user endpoints. In fact according to the August 2020 stats provided by Net Market Share[2], 87.6% of all computers run some version of Windows. At the time of writing this book, Windows 10 and Windows Server 2019 are the latest iterations of the popular operating system. However, Windows

---

[1]https://enterprise.verizon.com/resources/reports/dbir/
[2]https://netmarketshare.com/

Servers 2012 and 2016 and Windows 7, 8, and 8.1 are still prevalent in many homes and businesses. And herein lies the problem. As new operating systems are released, the older OSs are no longer maintained by Microsoft. Table 4-4 shows a snapshot of Windows OS version market share according to Net Market Share for August 2020, depicted alongside the "End of Support" date according to Microsoft.

Table 4-4. *Windows Net Market Share with End of Support Dates*

OS Version	Net Market Share for August 2020	End of Support Date
Windows 10	56.4%	Actively Supported
Windows 8.1	3.2%	January 10, 2023
Windows 7	26%	January 14, 2020
Windows XP	1.3%	April 8, 2014

According to the data, 27.3% of all Windows users are working on a version that is no longer supported by Microsoft. That means no more security patches or help desk support for enterprise customers. The fact that there are still thousands of Windows XP users in the wild is terrifying. If you're one of them, UPGRADE NOW! These stats are important as they show the number of targetable systems for cyber criminals and script kiddies around the world.

Okay, we covered why Windows is targeted, but how are they targeted. As previously stated, 90% of all malware comes in via email. Users clicking links or opening attachments cause more initial compromises than any other method. This is called phishing, and it's been around for as long as there's been email. Have you ever been asked to help a wealthy Nigerian prince by sending him $1000 with the promise of receiving millions in return? If you answered yes, count yourself among the millions of other users who received a version of the same email. Unfortunately, that scheme did trick many people into forking over their hard-earned money with no return on investment. Today, phishing has evolved into the number one malware delivery platform.

The other common method for a compromised Windows endpoint is weak passwords. If your Windows endpoint is listening for Remote Desktop Protocol sessions, there is a good chance you'll be targeted by a brute force attack sometime in your future. The strength of your password will determine how successful the attacker will be. When it comes to password complexity, there are two schools of thought. First, the longer the password is, the longer the brute force will take. And second, the more diverse the character set of the password, the longer the brute force will take. At the end of the day, both are true with one caveat. If you use words in your password, the easier it will be to guess. Modern password-cracking tools have the ability to ingest word lists and modify the letters by using modifier rulesets to lessen the time it takes to crack a password. Cracking passwords can be a fun, at-home experiment that any cybersecurity professional should learn to do. We suggest learning tools such as John the Ripper and Hashcat.

Note   Here is our legal disclaimer: stealing or actively attempting to log in to services with passwords of others is illegal. Do not attempt any hacking activity without expressed or written permission.

The final topic we'll cover on Windows security is user permissions. Most at-home Windows 10 users operate day to day as the local administrator of their endpoint, meaning they do not use a separate, nonadmin account for daily activities. At home, this practice is acceptable. When a company allows their workforce to operate as the local administrator accounts on their company endpoints, the risk of malware infection is much higher. Let's look at a scenario.

Josh is Director of Sales at Acme Brick Company (ABC). ABC Information Security team allows all users' local administrator accounts on their work laptops. Josh received an email from an old college buddy inviting Josh to join an alumni forum. Josh clicks the link and has become a victim of drive-by malware. The malware begins propagating across other systems in the company and soon spreads to every system on the Sales team at Cyber NOW Education.

What's the danger of having local administrator permissions in this scenario? Simply put, the malware completely owned Josh's system immediately upon infection. Comparably if Josh's account had user level permissions, the malware would be severely limited within the rights of that user. Another key point against local admin is the ability to elevate to system-level privileges. If an attacker gains system-level access, there is nothing on the endpoint that's safe.

MacOS

Apple's MacOS is being adopted by more and more companies as their endpoints of choice making it the second most popular OS in the wild. MacOS is currently on release 10.x and can be found in all of Apple's desktop and laptop products. MacOS is a proprietary flavor of Unix; this allows the OS to operate on lower system resources and provides greater user control. As of August 2020, MacOS owns 9.4% of the operating system market share. That might not sound like a lot, but that number translates into millions of individual Apple devices at homes and offices globally.

Many people will say that Apple devices are more secure due to the lack of malware. While it is true there is less malware that targets MacOS, that's not what makes MacOS more secure. Apple has taken endpoint security to the hardware layer with built-in security chips on the motherboard. These chips are dedicated to encrypting the file storage, ensuring a secure boot of the OS every time, and application runtime security. Other software-based technologies like execute disable (XD), address space layout randomization (ASLR), and system integrity protection (SIP) all work to ensure malware can't affect critical system files. Despite being a very secure platform, signature-based detection is not built into MacOS.

User permissions in MacOS are very similar to most modern Linux distributions. By default, the root user is disabled and cannot be accessed. Users in the administrator group have the ability to elevate their privileges as needed to conduct admin tasks on the local system.

Overall, Apple's MacOS is a great option for increased security in your enterprise environment. Most small businesses adopt Microsoft's Active Directory services as their authentication mechanism, so Windows devices make more sense. While there are identity managers that allow MacOS to join Active Directory, it usually calls for a high level of IT support and costs. The price for an Apple device also plays a large role in the fight for endpoint supremacy, leading most small- to middle-sized companies to choose Windows devices as they can be 75% cheaper than a comparable Apple device.

Unix/Linux

Unix and Linux have grown more popular over the last couple of decades as the open source community has increased in size, owning 2% of the market share in August 2020. We won't be covering the differences in Unix and Linux, but if you're interested, there is a great article on Opensource. com[3] that goes into the history and differences in the operating systems. The most important note to take away about Unix or Linux is how many different flavors or versions exist. Today's most common Linux distributions are derived from either Debian or Fedora. Most Unix/Linux distros are free to download and use, and we would encourage you to pick a flavor of Linux and start experimenting.

---

[3]https://opensource.com/article/18/5/differences-between-linux-and-unix

Unix/Linux devices are in more places than you would think. With the advent of the Internet of things (IoT), Unix/Linux have infiltrated their way into every home and office. Some of the older, more common office devices that run Unix/Linux are printers, A/V systems, and VoIP telephones. Today, all modern smart devices run some form of Unix/Linux under the hood. As the idea of a connected home or office has grown over the last decade, so have the increased number of attacks on the Internet of things. Botnets are the most common use of compromised IoT devices. In 2016, the Mirai botnet was used to cripple much of the online infrastructure in the eastern United States when attackers used it to perform a DDOS attack against the Dyn Company.

Attackers have been targeting Unix/Linux since the very beginning, but not with malware. The majority of compromised Unix/Linux hosts are due to misconfigurations in either the OS or the applications hosted on the system. The majority of all websites are running on a distribution of Linux; a simple misconfiguration in the web application could allow a would-be attacker to gain credentialed access to the underlying operating system.

But we're talking about endpoints. Even though the majority of the Internet's infrastructure relies on Unix/Linux, end users haven't fully adopted Linux as a personal operating system, largely in part to the difficulty in managing the OS. Today, we see the largest adoption of Linux as an endpoint OS in the cybersecurity and software development communities. The biggest challenge to any enterprise environment using Unix/Linux is managing the variety of distributions, despite the existence of tools that manage multiple Unix/Linux distros.

Much like MacOS, malware does exist for Unix/Linux but not widespread. Also the user permissions are basically the same, since MacOS is based on the Linux kernel. Most commonly, Unix/Linux systems are compromised by the tools and packages installed on the system. Many Linux distributions come with a preinstalled programming language like Python.

Python is a very powerful toolset that allows administrators and developers to code out some pretty impressive tasks. Unfortunately, the functionality that makes Python a power admin tool also makes it a favorite toolset for attackers. Python's popularity has skyrocketed over the last several years, and we would suggest adding Python courses to your "to-do" list.

However, Python isn't the only language of its type. Every year, there are new scripting languages released, and every one of them can be used to compromise a system. Early on in my career, I (Jarrett) learned of an esoteric programming language that uses spaces, tabs, and new lines as its programming syntax. This language was called Whitespace; it was developed in 2003 by Edwin Brady and Chris Morris. With the number of programming languages in the wild, no one is expected to know them all. I've found the best method is to pick one language and dedicate yourself to it. Learning one will help you interpret most of the others when you see it in use.

Other Endpoints

We've covered the three largest categories of operating systems for endpoint devices, but there are some honorable mentions we should cover; we'll start with mobile devices. According to GSMA Intelligence's 2020 State of Mobile Internet Connectivity Report,[4] 3.8 billion people are using mobile Internet. That is almost half of the world's population. These mobile devices include cell phones, cellular-enabled tablets, and cars with built-in Wi-Fi hotspots. Mobile devices come in a few flavors of operating systems; they are Android, iOS, and Linux. Just like the endpoint discussion above, the vulnerabilities for Unix/Linux are shared with Android/Linux mobile OS. iOS, however, is a bit more secure. This is due

---

[4]https://data.gsmaintelligence.com/research/research/research-2020/
the-state-of-mobile-internet-connectivity-report-2020

to the limitations that Apple has placed on their user's ability to install untrusted, third-party software. This is called the "walled garden" strategy. If you control the application distribution platform, you can ensure that dangerous software never makes it onto your device.

Let's talk about the Internet of things or IoT devices; odds are you have these in your home already. This is an all-encompassing term for smart devices. The biggest risk to IoT devices is unsecured OS holes. Since the majority of IoT devices are unmanaged, we place a lot of faith in the developers who made the product. There are countless white papers and articles on IoT devices with security vulnerabilities. If you have a smart device, you should research their vulnerabilities on websites such as Exploit-db.com and Mitre.org.

The final endpoint device we'll cover is the Chromebook by Google. This is a very low-cost solution for the laptop market. The Chromebook is running a custom flavor of Linux known as ChromeOS, based on the Gentoo Linux distribution. Google has stated that ChromeOS is the most secure OS on the market. Regardless of how true that claim might be, the system is only as secure as the apps installed. Google has taken efforts to limit the apps installed on their system, but there are methods of circumventing these protections.

Summary

We covered a lot in this chapter. We started off talking about networking, and the key to remember here is to make sure you know the difference between a public and a private network. RFC1918 governs the Internet for what is considered a private network address space. It is important to know! We also covered common port numbers. It is common to get a pop quiz in a SOC analyst interview to ask you what port number matches which service.

The items that we want you to make sure you remember from network security are that firewalls draw the imaginary circle around your private Internet address space and define the **perimeter**. If you know what a private IP and public IP address is, you can visualize if it goes inside the perimeter or outside of the perimeter, and firewalls create the boundary.

Note   There is a concept in networking called Network Address Translation (NAT) that allows public IP addresses to communicate with private IP addresses using a NAT table. This would be a great concept to study on your own.

For user endpoints there are three major categories for endpoint security: Windows, which has the lion's share of market, MacOS, which has a growing market share, and Unix/Linux, which come in third. Additionally, there are mobile and IoT devices to consider in a separate bucket as far as security is concerned.

CHAPTER 5

The SOC Analyst

In this chapter, we'll discuss the tools to be aware of as a SOC analyst, concepts to understand, common security definitions, and zero trust infrastructure.

Imagine badging into the front door of your office building and saying hello to the guard that you see every day, wondering what you will get him for Christmas. You leave your badge at home, more often than you should, so you've chitchatted a bit as he gets you a temporary badge. You know he has a little boy about to turn two, and he really likes hot wheels. You think about this as you tell him to have a nice day, and you approach the elevator to go to your floor. You badge the elevator to get to your floor, because your floor is locked unless you are approved to get in. Then you walk more toward the center of the floor where the SOC sits, and you badge one more door to get to the common areas and where the sales and engineering teams sit in their cubicles. As you approach the center of the room, there are two doors within feet from each other. This is called a mantrap, and it allows security to trap someone in between the two doors for them to be escorted out of the building. You swipe your badge the first door, and then briefly you get a little anxiety if the locks broke or my badge suddenly didn't work that you'd be trapped in the mantrap in some kind of horror experiment. You try your badge again and make it through to the heart of security: the Security Operations Center! It is dark and there are windows, but there are blinds covering all of the windows. It is eerie because the only time the blinds seemed to be opened are to let the window cleaners clean

© Tyler Wall and Jarrett Rodrick 2021
T. Wall and J. Rodrick, *Jump-start Your SOC Analyst Career*,
https://doi.org/10.1007/978-1-4842-6904-6_5

the windows. You look above your head around you, and you instantly are brought to the front lines as the TVs that line the ceiling are displaying what is going on in your global company, and in the world in real time. You are sucked into your role, and you say hello to your friends and then jump into action.

Note   This was an actual SOC for a Managed Security Services Provider that we worked for. They would periodically bring clients in to show them how serious they took security. It sometimes felt like being watched like fish in a tank, but it made me feel pride in what I was doing.

Tools

The number one tool you will need to know as a security analyst in this decade is what a Security Incident and Event Management (SIEM) tool is and how it plays into your role. The SIEM is the heartbeat of the SOC. Everything that is done on a device can generate a log. Without logs there would not be a security analyst. Without logs there would not be security. When devices from all around the world generate logs, the idea is to send it to a single point where all of the logs can be observed and measured. This concept is called a "single pane of glass" and is ideally the one screen that the SOC can operate without having to chain multiple web browsers and sites together to accomplish the review of security events. The single pane of glass is the SIEM.

SIEM

Other than collecting logs, the SIEM also normalizes logs, which means to put them into the correct chronological order. Because of the varying time zones across the world configured in your devices, the timestamps, or date and time, on each log need to be accounted for. Also in normalization, when the logs are ingested into the SIEM platform, they must meet a certain standard and format.

Each SIEM has a "special sauce" or proprietary technique that is used to take in billions of logs and picks out the things that are suspicious, but at a basic level, either the vendor or the users (or both) create rules that if any of the logs match a given criteria, it will sound the alarm. Next-generation SIEM platforms perform User Entity and Behavior Analytics (UEBA) which attempts to monitor all of your users (not log) and create a baseline of activity that is considered normal and then sound the alarm when someone is outside of that normal activity.

Also in next-generation SIEM platforms, they are moving toward being a case manager as well. When there are multiple alarms that are seemingly related, they offer a way to combine them and track evidence and investigations in a way that is meaningful and easy to be used.

Lastly in next-generation SIEM platforms, they are moving toward integration automation. Security Orchestration, Automation, and Response (SOAR) is rapidly gaining traction in the industry and is poised to be the next "single pane of glass." SIEM vendors and buying SOAR platforms that are more mature and bringing them into their product, or building their own capabilities in their product but at the very basic level it allows predefined playbooks to be ran automatically for common security issues which frees you up to work on the more challenging and more interesting items.

Note   At the time of writing, a few SIEM vendors of note are Splunk, Elastic, LogRhythm, QRadar, and FortiSIEM. Two of the more mature SOAR platforms are Demisto and Splunk Phantom.

Firewalls

Additional to SIEM and SOAR, you will likely come across firewalls. Firewall and firewall engineering is a specialty all on its own, but it's important jargon to understand the biggest players in the firewall space are Cisco, Checkpoint, Fortinet, Palo Alto, Juniper, and SonicWall. As a security analyst, you might be responsible for performing a firewall block on an IP address, or requesting to have it done. What this means is you have used the tools and techniques of a security analyst and determined that it was bad, and you want to block that IP address from being communicated with from your internal network.

IDS/IPS

You will also need to know what an intrusion prevention system (IPS) and an intrusion detection system (IDS) is. A "protection" system allows actions to be taken by the device as they happen to control the flow of network activity. A "detection" system only allows for it to be detected, and not to interject with actions. Most IPSs can act as IDSs and vice versa, and the main difference is where it is put on the network. IDS/IPS can be either host based or network based. Some other acronyms you might come across are HIPS/HIDS and NIPS/NIDS. Figure 5-1 is a basic illustration of two computers communicating and how the IDS would fit in, just monitoring passively.

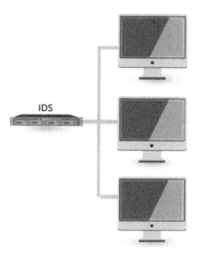

Figure 5-1. *Intrusion Detection System*

Intrusion detection systems can either be placed in line or through a network tap, as seen in Figure 5-1. Intrusion detection systems are designed to detect and not take preventative measures. Tapping the network allows the device to see the network traffic but not affect bandwidth. IDS placed through a tap cannot take preventative action because they cannot control the flow of traffic.

Figure 5-2 depicts two computers communicating and how an IPS would fit into the network in an active scenario. The IPS has the ability to change the flow of traffic between the two devices because of the way it sits on the network.

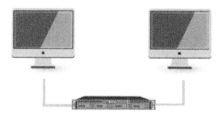

Figure 5-2. *Intrusion Protection System*

Intrusion prevention systems must be placed as seen in Figure 5-2. Placing an IPS in line allows it to control the flow of traffic and take preventative actions to protect.

IDS can be placed in line as well. Most modern IPS will have some rules set to "take action" and some set to monitor only. These are called intrusion detection and prevention systems (IDPS).

Sandboxing

Another tool you may come cross is a sandbox. When you hear someone say, "Did you sandbox that?", what they mean is have you executed the file or website in a protected environment to find out what it does. Quite a few endpoint detection softwares will detonate the file on your behalf so it can know whether it is bad or not, but nothing comes as close as a good report from Cuckoo, Hybrid Analysis, or Joe Sandbox. These tools are designed to twist every knob and press every button to squeeze as much execution information as they can out of it. As a SOC analyst, you mainly use these tools to get out indicators of compromise like hashes of files that it drops, or IP addresses and domains it contacts to run these through your SIEM to see if there are any historical connections.

There are a few online sandbox tools, but be wary to now execute proprietary files in a public sandbox to be shared with the community. Other online tools to take note of are:

- **Virustotal.com:** VirusTotal is perhaps the most useful online tool to a SOC analyst. You visit the website and punch in a URL or hash, and you will, most of the time, have a good idea if the IoC is good or bad.

- **Domain Tools:** The whois tool at domain tools I always found very easy to use. While there are plenty of very good online whois searches available, I always like to use domain tools.

- **Talos Intelligence:** Use this tool to conduct reputational checks on IP addresses and URLs.

- **IPVoid:** Use this tool to check blacklists for a particular IP address.

- **URLVoid:** Use this tool to check URLs for safety reputations.

- **Threat Crowd:** Use this tool as a search engine for threats. Threat Crowd is a system for finding and researching artifacts relating to cyber threats.

- **TOR Exit Node List:** Check to see if the IP address is on a TOR exit node.

- **IBM X-Force Exchange:** Check the IoC for information in X-Force Exchange.

- **Search Engine:** Always check a search engine when looking for suspicious items. Some gems are more hidden!

Note   A search engine like Google cannot be understated in importance for an analyst. Yes, you have all of these tools, but sometimes you might Google an indicator and come across someone's personal blog who has completed a complete reverse engineering of the malware. You would have never found it if you didn't Google!

Definitions

As you go through your day as a SOC analyst, you will come across terms that aren't always agreed on, and the meanings are a bit vague. From the best of our combined experience, these are the best definitions for these terms. Figure 5-3 is a chart of the order of volume from each class.

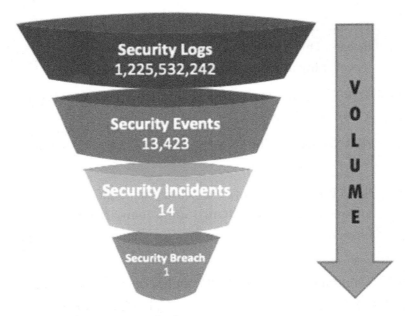

Figure 5-3. *Volume Funnel Chart*

Security Logs: Most Common

At the very base of a security program are security logs. These logs could be from anything and everything and about anything and everything. Once they are ingested into a SIEM, they become a security log. An example of important security logs that a SOC would want to capture are network flow logs, Windows Event Logs, Unix Syslogs, and firewall logs. Security events can string together many security logs.

Security Event: Common

Security events are the day-to-day routine security monitoring from the tooling. They are very common, and almost all security tooling notifications start as a security event generated from security logs, with the exception of vulnerability scanners, and are escalated as needed. A security event must be escalated to a security incident before becoming a breach. When a security event is escalated to become an incident, the incident response process triggers, and an incident handler is assigned.

Incident: Uncommon

Security incidents are uncommon but happen more frequently than a security breach. An incident is declared, and the incident response process starts if there is **suspected** loss of sensitive data.

What is not an incident: security events and vulnerabilities that have not been escalated.

Security Breaches: Rare

Security breaches are rare and contain a **verified loss of data containing sensitive personal information**. In most cases to utter the words something is a breach, it requires the legal department and the CISO to declare a breach. As a new analyst, it is good practice to not use this term anywhere unless told otherwise. In most cases, breaches require a breach notification to clients and sometimes the public and are handled with extra sensitivity.

All breaches start as incidents.

Summary

When you start your new job on day one, it will help you tremendously if you even have heard of some of these technologies, not to mention how much it will help you to understand them during the interview process. As I stated, the SIEM is the most important tool today to know as a SOC analyst. In the future, more single panes of glass are going to be driven by SOAR platforms, but they will likely be a combined product – A SIEM/SOAR product as a single pane of glass.

CHAPTER 6

SOC in the Clouds

This chapter was contributed by Anand Purohit.

This chapter will discuss what cloud computing is, the major vendors of cloud computing, and how cloud security differs.

What Is Cloud Computing?

According to the NIST, "Cloud computing is a model for enabling ubiquitous and on-demand network access to a shared pool of configurable computing resources (e.g., networks, servers, storage, applications, and services) that can be rapidly provisioned and released with minimal management effort or service provider interaction."[1]

If we simplify this definition, what cloud computing provides is an operating model to deliver services (compute, storage, network, databases, platforms, and applications) as a layered set of abstractions on top the usual data center basic building blocks of racks, servers, arrays of magnetic and solid-state storage, and networks.

Cloud computing differs from traditional computing in that it is engineered, pooled, and managed at scale in a way to deliver lowest cost per service (compute/min. or storage/GB or data transfer/GB) using economies of scale.

---

[1]https://csrc.nist.gov/publications/detail/sp/800-145/final

© Tyler Wall and Jarrett Rodrick 2021
T. Wall and J. Rodrick, *Jump-start Your SOC Analyst Career*,
https://doi.org/10.1007/978-1-4842-6904-6_6

Cloud can be deployed within an organization-owned or leased data centers and managed by internal IT called private cloud, or it can be consumed over the Internet/VPN (or a dedicated connection) from a CSP (cloud service provider like AWS, Google GCP, Microsoft Azure, etc.).

Figure 6-1 shows a typical cloud-layered structure.

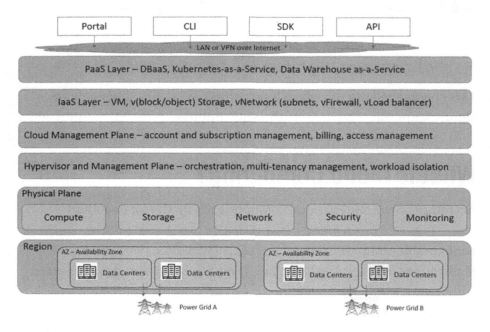

Figure 6-1. *Layered Stack Representation of Cloud*

Once the deployment model is selected (private or public), cloud computing can be used in one of many service forms such as infrastructure, platform, or software.

Types of Cloud Computing Deployment Models

Cloud computing is popularly deployed in three popular ways, public cloud, private cloud, and hybrid cloud:

Public Cloud: Owned and operated by a cloud provider like AWS, Microsoft Azure, or Google GCP and consumed by enterprises and individuals using a pay-as-you-go billing model.

Private Cloud: Owned and operated by an enterprise in its own or colo. data center offering infrastructure and application platforms to its internal consumers and developers, some enterprises do create a charge-back or showback pricing model internally to recover the cost of running the private cloud across all business units.

Hybrid Cloud: Hybrid cloud is one of the most loosely used cloud deployment models in the industry. Broadly speaking it can be divided into two types:

- Proprietary hybrid cloud Stack

- Siloed hybrid cloud

Examples of proprietary single-vendor hybrid cloud stack would be AWS Outpost, Microsoft Azure Stack, VMC (VMware of Cloud), and Google's Anthos (although Anthos is capable of also running on top of other public/private cloud IaaS such as AWS, Azure, or VMware, hence it's a hybrid and multicloud proprietary solution designed as a kubernetes control plane).

Examples of siloed hybrid cloud deployment model would be an organization using a public cloud provider like AWS, Azure, or GCP and pairing it with a mature private cloud deployment in its own data centers like VMware and OpenStack. Now, these two silos of public and private clouds can operate separately with its own management planes, or they can be front ended with a third-party management plane called CMP (cloud management platform) from companies like RightScale (Flexera), Scalr, and Cisco Cloud Center.

Figure 6-2 shows the evolution of proprietary hybrid cloud solutions from three leading cloud providers.

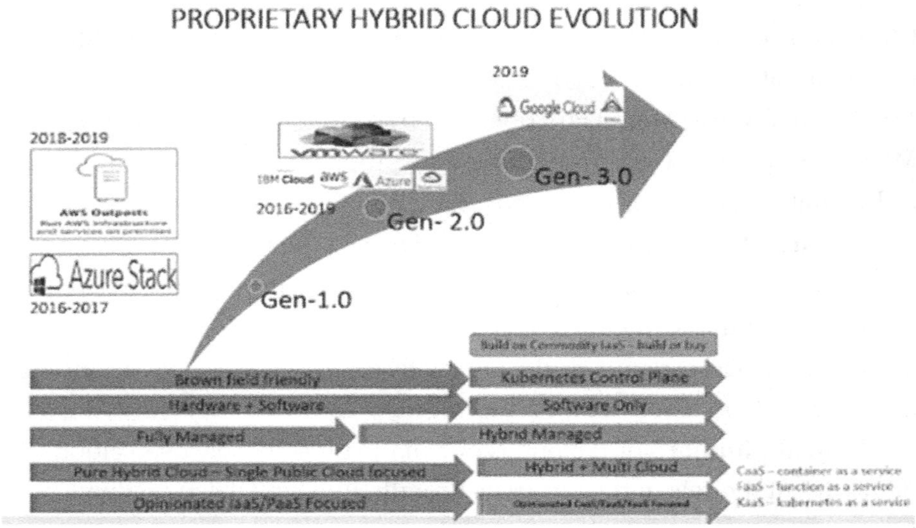

Figure 6-2. *Proprietary Hybrid Cloud Stack*

Multicloud: Another cloud deployment model used in the industry is multicloud, which can be considered as a cloud deployment model consisting of multiple clouds (private, public, or both) being managed separately using their respective management plane or front ended with a CMP (cloud management platform). The biggest difference between multicloud and hybrid cloud is the fact that hybrid cloud will always have private cloud as one of the participating clouds, but multicloud is a more generic term.

Cloud Service Models

Although there are many cloud service models, the four most broad categories are as follows:

Infrastructure as a Service (IaaS): When the cloud deployment (public or private) is used to offer infrastructure components like compute (VM), storage (block, object, file), and networks (virtual network, subnets, virtual load balancer – network or application).

Platform as a Service (PaaS): When the cloud deployment (public or private) is used to offer some kind of a development platform which can be used to deploy binaries and develop data applications or stores.

Examples would be Google App Engine (public, code deployment), AWS Elastic Beanstalk (public, code deployment), Azure App Service (public, code deployment), Heroku (public, code deployment), Cloud Foundry (private, code deployment), and AWS Redshift (public, data mart development)

PaaS can be further classified into:

- **Database as a Service (DBaaS):** AWS RDS, DynamoDB, Azure SQL, etc.

- **Data Warehouse as a Service (DWaaS):** AWS Redshift, Snowflake, and GCP BigQuery

- **Kubernetes as a Service (KaaS):** Kubernetes (application deployment and execution platform) as a service like AWS EKS, Azure AKS, and GCP GKP

Desktop as a Service (DaaS) (IaaS + PaaS): Desktop as a service delivers managed VDI (virtual desktop infrastructure) as a service over the network examples are AWS WorkSpaces, Microsoft Azure DaaS, VMware Horizon Cloud, and Citrix Managed Desktops.

Software as a Service (SaaS): When the cloud deployment is used to offer fully executed applications (vs. development building blocks as in IaaS or PaaS) via web portal, cli, or api, it's called SaaS like Salesforce for CRM, Workday for HCM, and Microsoft Office 365 for office productivity suite.

Evolution: Virtualization to Early Days of Cloud

Although the concept of aggregating large pool of compute resources and allowing it to be shared remotely using a "time-sharing" scheduler has been around since the 1950s during the Mainframe era, the modern-day cloud computing as we know can be credit to developments in hardware virtualization or what is often called VMM (virtual machine manager/ monitor also known as the hypervisor).[2]

A hypervisor is a software that emulated the hardware (CPU, RAM, hard drive, NIC card, floppy drive, etc.) and helps create virtual machines (software abstractions of a server or desktop) and manage resources like physical CPU, memory, storage, and network as a pool that can be easily reallocated between virtual machine abstractions running on it.

Hypervisor as a software has a lot of operating system–type components like memory manager, process scheduler, input/output (I/O) stack, device drivers, and a network stack (and more) to run VMs.

This exact concept that was introduced in VMM or hypervisor (abstraction, pooling, and orchestration of resources) when applied across storage, network (network virtualization), monitoring, and security forms the foundations for the modern-day cloud computing.

Three parallel streams of developments were going on in the industry during early 2000 to 2010 which contributed to the mainstream cloud adoption.

---

[2]U.S. Patent 6,397,242 by VMware in 1998, http://patft.uspto.gov/netacgi/ nph-Parser?patentnumber=6,397,242

Era of Virtualization

Companies like Microsoft and VMware were both focusing of hypervisor-enabled product rollout that offered hardware virtualization and virtual machine management.

Microsoft acquired Virtual PC for Windows from Connectix, and VMware released a series of products including VMware Player, VMware Server, VMware Workstation, ESX, and GSX both focused on offering a hosted hypervisor (also called type 2 hypervisor) for running DeskOS (Windows 98, 2000, XP, Win7) and ServerOS (Windows Server 2003, Server 2008, Linux).

These developments were geared toward enabling enterprises to use their own underutilized and unutilized pool of compute, storage, and network resources in the data center as abstracted virtual services, thus increasing efficiency and reducing cost.

These early developments in virtualization laid the foundations for Microsoft's private (Hyper-V) and public (Azure) cloud as well as VMware's private cloud portfolio (vSphere)

Early Cloud Development

When Microsoft and VMware were focusing on enabling enterprise to leverage abstracted computing services internally within their data centers, some new entrants like Amazon, Google, and Heroku were looking at using similar abstraction on top of their infrastructure/data centers to offer orchestrated services to external consumers over the Internet, which eventually became public cloud.

Amazon launched IaaS - EC2 (Elastic Compute Cloud) as one of its first clouds offering under the umbrella AWS (Amazon Web Services) in 2006.

Google announced Google App Engine (GAE) in 2008, a platform for developing and hosting web applications in Google-managed data centers (what is now categorized under the umbrella of PaaS – platform as a service) followed by Google cloud storage in 2010 and GCE (Google Compute Engine) IaaS in 2012.

Heroku also started in 2007 as one of the first public cloud PaaS offering developers to build, run, and scale applications across many languages. (Heroku was acquired by Salesforce in 2010.)

Open Source Hypervisors and Cloud Development

While the proprietary technology giants such as Microsoft and VMware were focusing on closed source licensed hypervisors (Hyper-V, ESX), open source also developed its variants.

In 2003, first open source x86 hypervisor was released named Xen by the University of Cambridge as a research project. Amazon EC2 currently utilizes a highly customized version of the Xen hypervisor. Founders of Xen also created a company named XenSource which was acquired by Citrix and powers two of its leading products in the market of VDI (virtual desktop infrastructure), which is simply an abstraction and broker to deliver virtualized desktop OS (e.g., Windows 7, Windows 10) as VMs.

KVM (Kernel-based Virtual Machine) released in 2006 and eventually merged into the Linux kernel in 2007 is the second most significant open source hypervisor to be aware of; it's a virtualization module in the Linux kernel that allows the kernel to function as a hypervisor.

In 2008, NASA released its first open source cloud software stack named Nebula followed by a joint open source cloud software initiative with Rackspace known as OpenStack Project.

OpenStack promised enterprises a "Linux of private cloud" with no-vendor proprietary closed source lock-in and open ecosystem of providers to choose from including Red Hat, Mirantis, and SUSE.

Around 2010, the battle for private cloud supremacy was booming with OpenStack promising a no-vendor lock-in cloud software stack.

VMware on the other hand offered its flagship product vSphere (a combination of ESXi hypervisor and vCenter management suite of products) as a private cloud which had the most mature, hardened, and enterprise-grade features.

Microsoft also evolved its Virtual PC product into a full-blown server virtualization/private cloud product named Hyper-V as part of its Windows Server 2008 release which was later complemented with System Center Virtual Machine Manager (SCVMM) as the management layer (similar to vCenter in VMware product suite).

Microsoft's public cloud first step was launched in 2008 (2 years after AWS's first cloud product EC2) as project Red Dog followed by release of Windows Azure in 2010 which was later renamed to Microsoft Azure to reflect Microsoft holistic cloud strategy across Office 365 (SaaS) and Dynamic CRM.

Cloud Security

A popular phrase in cloud security says "The provider is responsible for the security OF the cloud and consumer is responsible for the security IN the cloud." This is the general rule of thumb and an important understanding of the fundamental cybersecurity model in the cloud.

We have overlaid the same cloud diagram from earlier in this chapter to show the clear responsibility boundary when it comes to cloud security in Figure 6-3.

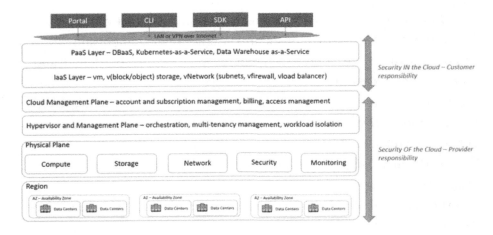

Figure 6-3. *Shared Cloud Security Model*

This is also referred to as "Shared Responsibility Model" or "Shared Security Model" in the industry where the cloud provider CSP is responsible for the security of physical data centers, asset and host access, servers, physical network, storage devices, hypervisor, and management plane security.

CSPs also provide cloud native security control implementation methods and tools like IAM, infrastructure and network logs, data protection services like encryption, KMS, certificate management, security event management, and log analytics.

CSP also provides independent audit evidence for customers to meet their regulatory and compliance requirements when hosting regulated applications and data in cloud.

When thinking of public cloud security, an organization should think of it as a stacked layer of security controls building on top of each other depending on the type of service consumed.

Foundationally, one should first build a solid IAM, network security, data protection, and management plane security.

Next, it should build layers of additional security services and controls based on the service delivery type (IaaS, PaaS, SaaS), threat exposure, classification of the data the service will interact with, regulations, and compliance attached to the data hosted.

The last piece of security is the workload or application security which can be consumed from the cloud provider's native tools, or the customer can bring their third-party tool and host it on the CSP's IaaS or VMs.

At each layer of these building blocks, you would need engineering (to build consumable products using the cloud provider's native services or third-party vendor solutions) and operations (to provide day 2 and beyond lifecycle management).

One of the simplest ways to categorize most (not all) cloud providers' native security services is to layer them according to the class of security capability it maps to, as shown in Figure 6-4.

Security Management

| Managed SEIM and Aggregator | Governance Policy Engine | Threat detection service |

Logs and Metrics security

| Service logs | Network flow logs | API logs | Log Analytics Managed Service |

Data security

| Keys management service(KMS) | Certificate manager | HSM – Hardware security module |

Identity security

| Identity and access management | Secrets management | Managed directory services |

Infrastructure security

| Isolated virtual network segments | Firewall | Secure Gateway | Web Application Firewall/DDoS |

Figure 6-4. *Cloud Provider Native Security Services*

These services can also be classified or grouped into the five stages of security as defined by NIST, i.e., Identify, Protect, Detect, Respond, and Recover.

The most practical reality when it comes to cloud security is that it's highly dynamic in many aspects, such as

- The number of cloud services to protect (e.g., AWS as of Nov 2020 has 175 services) keeps increasing every year.

- Growing number of threats.

- Constantly changing compute and network stack for AI/ML (e.g., GPU/TPU, IaaS, and networks moving from 10G to 25G, 40G, and 100G networks).

- Rapidly changing compute abstractions requiring rethinking of both infrastructure and application security (e.g., containers and serverless/FaaS).

Conclusion

Cloud has definitely lowered the barrier for entry for new entrants across industries causing disruption in business models resulting in organizations either trying to replicate similar frictionless technology provider model in house (private cloud) or moving toward a public cloud to provide seamless technology services as an API endpoint.

This is a win-win for both since organizations do not have to perform technology and data center capacity planning, procurement, and lifecycle management but rather consume IT as a service and just focus on the core business which could be healthcare, finance, or retail.

This ease of consumption model with cloud also comes with a set of challenges and learning curve for organization in terms of cultural shift, change management, process, and skillset management.

Organizations need to promote constant learning and rapid experimentation rebuild legacy technology processes that worked during data center days including security, risk, compliance, and audit process.

CHAPTER 7

SOC Automation

This chapter was contributed by Jason Tunis.

This chapter will discuss the maturity models of Security Operations Centers, how to know where your SOC is at, and how to embrace SOC automation and stay ahead of the curve.

Automation within the Security Operations Center (SOC) is generally referred to as Security Automation and Orchestration (SAO) or Security Automation, Orchestration, and Response (SOAR). As an analyst it has become increasingly more common to encounter some type of security automation within organizations. To what extent may depend on the maturity of your organization and its SOC. We will dive into maturity models and how those relate to automation a bit later in this chapter. First, what is security automation?

What Is SOC Automation?

No, SOC automation does not refer to robots becoming self-aware. Threat intelligence feeds do not suggest that "judgment day" is close on the horizon. Simply stated, automation is the machine implementation of low-level security-related actions. These actions are small pieces of a larger task. Generally, a task will be made from a number of actions. Similarly, a process will encompass a number of tasks. Tasks can be partially or fully automated with the goal of reducing human intervention in security operations. Orchestration, while very closely tied to automation, takes

© Tyler Wall and Jarrett Rodrick 2021
T. Wall and J. Rodrick, *Jump-start Your SOC Analyst Career*,
https://doi.org/10.1007/978-1-4842-6904-6_7

advantage of multiple automation tasks across multiple systems or platforms. Orchestration is used to automate or semiautomate more complex workflows and processes.

We have heard criticism from SOC analysts and others in the security community regarding automation. The overwhelming theme seems to be that analysts are worried that automation will take their job. At first glance I can see where they are coming from. If a machine can do it faster and more efficiently, then what is the analyst to do? Believe me, I get it! As a SOC lead, I want to challenge my analysts to do a detailed analysis of events. This takes a good amount of time and is not possible with the volume of events seen on a daily basis. I want them to look for trends, examine data over a larger period of time, and then find the reason that these events are taking place. To ask themselves questions like: "Is the reason I have to respond to 50 events per day on an IPS signature due to the fact that the webserver is vulnerable?". Present that data back to your SOC leadership, and take initiative to get the business to patch the vulnerability.

What we are attempting to convey is that SOC automation should not be seen as a limitation to your career, rather a springboard which can help you become a better analyst. We will go over a number of reasons for automation in the next section that should paint a clearer picture of the benefit of automation not only to the SOC but to the individual analysts as well. Let's dig into why automation is a positive addition to any SOC.

Why Automate?

There are a number of reasons for a SOC to automate, but be assured that replacing analysts is generally not the goal. The SOC analyst is a valuable resource which will always be needed to perform where machines cannot. Whether part of a maturity initiative or new business requirements, leadership is often left taking on additional services with the same or fewer resources. Taking into account that SOC leadership is being pressured to deliver more, combined with the shortage of skilled cybersecurity professionals, it is easy to see why automation is a no-brainer.

I have spent time in the trenches working through an endless queue of events. When I was a junior analyst, there were times when I would have a number of events that were generated for antivirus detections where the files were quarantined. Over half of the events in that day were "potentially unwanted applications" (PUA) which were adware/toolbar related. The tool did its job, the files were quarantined, yet I still had a number of events that needed to be addressed. I had to manually add the appropriate notes and close each ticket. If I had automation in place, then it would have made my life a lot easier. I would have been able to focus on more in-depth analysis and look for a common source of the adware, but due to the sheer volume of events, it was not an option at that time.

For me, automation is a force multiplier when it comes to helping analysts with the flood of events they handle on a daily basis. I wish I had more analysts in the SOC. By eliminating the need for analysts to do monotonous tasks, they are free to spend more time performing higher-level analysis of events. Senior analysts will have more time to dedicate to train junior analysts. More time can be spent on developing documentation, and with the ever-changing pace of a SOC, we all know this is always needed.

One of the first reasons a SOC may choose to automate is to streamline existing processes. Many SOAR platforms have C-level dashboards that are designed to show the amount of time and money saved by automating actions. While I do agree to an extent that this can be important, focusing on this alone may not necessarily the best fit for all organizations. There are a number of reasons that I believe are equally important to the operation of a healthy SOC.

One of my favorite reasons for automating is to reduce analyst fatigue. I cannot be the only analyst that has ever spent what seems like hours a day pressing "Ctrl+C" and "Ctrl+V." I have gone home at the end of the day with brain fried, wondering if a monkey could do the job just as well. As I mentioned earlier, security analysts are the most important resource that a SOC has. These analysts are inundated day-in and day-out with an abundance of information that needs to be collected, categorized, classified, analyzed, and interpreted. Reducing the volume of events that need to be analyzed is one way to achieve this.

Reducing analyst fatigue benefits the SOC by reducing overall stress and making it a fun and challenging place to work. Isn't the saying: "Happy SOC, Happy Life"? Good leadership should strive to do all that they can to promote morale and a healthy workplace environment. Doing the same repetitive actions day-in and day-out will desensitize you and cause you to skip steps or cut corners. This fatigue increases the possibility for mistakes to be made.

Reducing mistakes leads me to another popular reason for automating which is standardizing processes. Analysts can get trapped in an endless screen-switching cycle during an investigation by checking documentation, following defined steps, and moving between multiple consoles. When automating security-related tasks, we drive consistency and reduce the likelihood for errors. Consistency is key in security operations. During incident response when we implement automation, we can ensure that processes are consistently followed.

As a SOC analyst, it is very easy to cast wide nets in order to collect as much information as possible. Sometimes the rules we write just need to be broad. The events generated by a rule may only be an indicator when correlated to another event or other condition. Sure, you could write a correlation rule, but maybe you are in the infancy of tuning a rule, and thus analysts receive a large number of false-positive detections. What if we could use automation to tune out these false positives? Reducing the overall volume of false positives is one such use case that I have spent a good amount of time automating. I will give an example of this later in the chapter. (See example #1.)

Each analyst has their own preference for sources of information, and this can sometimes create false positives or lead an analyst down the wrong rabbit hole. As mentioned above, consistency is important for a number of reasons, but in addition to those already mentioned, another reason to automate is for the reduction of information bias. There are some reputation and intelligence data sharing services that are higher fidelity than others. Open source feeds can be a double-edged sword. On one side they may have larger reference sets and are good quality, but on the other side, I have found that it is easier for one wrong attribution to skew a full dataset. When the sources for which data is ingested and consumed are defined by the team, reputation checking and intelligence enrichment can be easily automated within your playbooks.

Every few months, it seems like there is a new attack pattern and threats are becoming more complex each and every day. Organizations need to be prepared for this evolution of complex threats. Adversaries today are utilizing automation to conduct attacks against your organization. Security operations need to keep up with the speed at which attackers are evolving, and the only way to do this is through automation and orchestration. As you implement new automation playbooks, the end goal should be to reduce the mean time to detection (MTTD) and mean time to response (MTTR). Each step that is automated shaves fractions of seconds from these SOC metrics. While at first glance it may not seem that a machine could save much time per single action, the culmination of all of these small actions over time will add up to significant time savings. The decrease of these metrics will satisfy senior management while also providing the numerous benefits mentioned previously.

SOC Maturity

I would like to preface this section by stating that I do not think many organizations would expect that they could fully automate every process from beginning to end. I believe there are just so many situations that require an analyst to make a decision that a machine just cannot do. There have been many horror stories of automation putting blocks in place based upon the wrong classification of the data. These instances have had catastrophic effects on businesses and their reputations. Until an organization has a high confidence level with the data being provided, I would personally suggest adding in some checks and balances into automation processes. These checks and balances should require human interaction and approval before blocking controls are put in place. All of these steps can be built into your playbooks to ensure that you can not only take advantage of automation to the fullest extent possibly but also keep automation from taking an incorrect action.

The goal of this chapter is not to go into a deep dive on the topic of maturity models. There are a few different ways to go about measuring the maturity of your SOC. You can write your own framework or use an industry standard framework to accomplish the same goal. The benefit to using a standardized framework is that it is recognized and probably being used by other organizations within your industry. Both solutions are designed to provide a situational summary of where the SOC is in their maturity taking into account all of its processes.

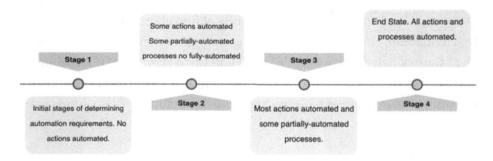

Figure 7-1. *Sample Maturity Phases*

When assessing the maturity of the SOC and its automation, it's easy enough to start with a staged approach similar to the one shown in Figure 7-1. I put this graphic together to illustrate that once you have completed an inventory of the processes and actions that your SOC is doing today, you can then map your current state and measure your progress toward your goals. Set small goals to get you to the next phase. If you have not begun your automation journey, don't be afraid of starting now. With each action you automate will get you closer to your goals.

As a junior analyst, you will begin to see areas for improvement in the processes that you and your team use every day. Document any process gaps and look for actions that can be automated. Take time to gather all of the appropriate data, and do the analysis. Can any of these actions be automated? What benefit do you see it providing the team? Be able to articulate how you believe automating an action will improve the function. By presenting a process improvement or resolution to a problem and not just the gap, you will set yourself as a leader among your peers, and SOC leadership will see you as a true problem solver.

How to Start Automating

There is no one-size-fits-all solution for every organization. In my experience it has been the most beneficial for analysts within the SOC that are intimately familiar with their processes and procedures to spend a little bit of time analyzing the work they perform each day. Categorize your tasks by the time required to complete them, and then by the complexity of the task. Start with the tasks that are simple, and do not take a lot of time to complete and leave the complex tasks for after you are comfortable with the process flow. Chances are that there are a number of these simple tasks, and by automating them you will make a good amount of progress. Figure 7-2 may help you categorize your tasks and allow you to focus on automation tasks that will provide the most value up front.

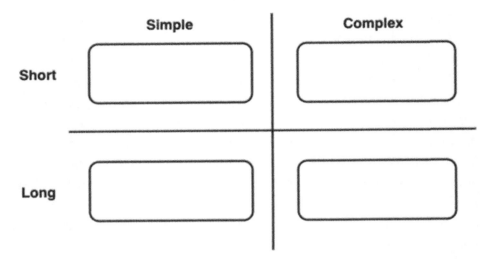

Figure 7-2. *Security Task Categorization*

When starting with a simple task that takes a short time to complete, look for repetitive actions without complex conditions. If you have different actions that you take based upon the output of an action, it will add complexity to the playbook. I have found that it is very easy to start working through a use case, only to find out halfway through it that one small attribute changes the full thing. Spend time dissecting the actions and whiteboard the process flow. Make every effort to break it down to the smallest steps that you can. A very simple example of automating a task such as this may be getting the reputation of a file. This might make it a bit easier to help you envision the steps taken.

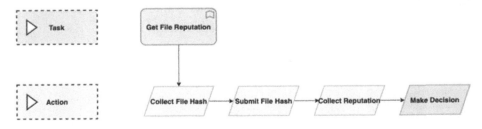

Figure 7-3. *Simple use case of getting a file reputation*

In this simple example, I have broken down the task into four small actions that an analyst would need to take:

1. Gather the file hash.

2. Open a web browser.

3. Paste the hash into the browser and submit it.

4. Make a decision based upon the file reputation.

The decision made upon the file reputation may then feed another action or a process flow further downstream. A playbook can be this small. Keep in mind that it is possible to have a playbook that calls other playbooks synchronously, waiting for the first one to complete before calling another.

At first glance it may not look like that by automating this task, you would save much time. What if the hash was a false-positive detection? What if we could automatically close the event based on the file reputation? What if we could collect the false-positive file and submit it back to the vendor to be reevaluated? Not only would automation help by eliminating the noise of false-positive detections, but it would reduce the number of tickets you would need to respond to. Now, this short, simple action has saved a significant amount of time when scaled to the number of events needed to be investigated in a day.

Sample Use Cases

I have come across a number of use cases discussed in different articles around the Web. Maybe some of them will work for you, or maybe they will just spark some ideas on what can be done. Like I mentioned earlier in this chapter, there is no one size fits all. Vendors supply sample playbooks that are generally meant as teaching points to what their product can do. Unfortunately, not every solution will be able to be integrated with your automation platform. You will encounter situations that may not work in your environment, just as you will also encounter situations that the vendor has not specifically encountered before. This is to be expected and is all a part of the journey of SOC automation. I wanted to highlight a couple use cases that I have personally encountered that I have had good success with. They do not cover every use case or reason that a SOC may choose to automate; however, they may act as a starting point or inspiration for your automation endeavors.

A use case that I have encountered was reducing a number of false-positive detections from an email hygiene provider. The team utilized a service that sends alerts for a malicious email that was delivered. There are times that when after the alert is sent, the email is reclassified as clean. I wrote an automation playbook that would call the email hygiene provider's API to check for the "false-positive" flag. If the alert was a false positive, an analyst ticket would not be created.

Another use case which is a bit more advanced was providing paging to on-call analysts when critical events came in. We started by defining the type of events that would cause an analyst to be paged out. Once that was complete, we began to figure out how to collect the on-call person and their page address. This took a bit of custom python code using a plug-in called "beautifulsoup." The playbook would scrape an intranet page and parse out the email address to page and send an alert to that analyst with the context of the critical event. Once that step was complete, the playbook would monitor a mailbox for a read-receipt for the page. If the page is not acknowledged within an hour, the playbook will send the same page to the on-call escalation point of contact.

The most common automation use case that I have helped to put in place is the enrichment of events with threat intelligence. In this environment, events are sent from the SIEM to the automation platform for processing, and a ticket is created in a temporary ticket queue. The playbook will extract out indicators such as file hash, file path, source and destination IP addresses, etc. Depending on the event type, these indicators are enriched from various sources that are predefined by the SOC. The data is used to populate notes in the event and add context to the event for the analyst that works it. Once all of this enrichment is complete, the playbook will move the ticket from the temporary queue to the SOC analyst queue. The reasons for moving it to the analyst queue after all the enrichment is done are to prevent a ticket state change and to ensure that any error checking added to the playbook complete first. I want the analyst to have all the data they need to make a decision on the event, instead of having only partially complete data.

Summary

Security automation is a tool that assists your SOC analysts and allows them to be more effective with their work. In my opinion it is not designed to be a replacement for an analyst. We invest in automation technology to make us more efficient at our jobs, and we are going to be required to make decisions where a machine cannot. I don't want to focus directly on best practices for writing automation playbooks, but more of the overall process and how it relates to the SOC. With that in mind, I want to leave you with a few tips for success.

If you have not already begun your automation journey, talk with your team about the benefits of security automation. Get everyone on board with the idea and comfortable with how you envision the playbooks working for the team:

- Do a full inventory of the tasks your SOC performs. Break them down the time required, and complexity to complete them.

- Define your use cases before automating any actions. Focus initially on tasks that are simple and can be completed quickly. This will provide you some quick wins.

- Don't write long complicated playbooks. Break them down to specific tasks as much as possible. You can use a parent playbook to call multiple child playbooks.

- Don't be afraid to challenge the status quo. When you start automating processes, you may discover a new and better way to do something. Embrace these efficiencies, and automation will show its value to your organization.

While security automation may be in its infancy, there is much that can be done to improve the operations within your SOC. I hope I was able to provide some insight into why you need to begin automating sooner than later. I have highlighted a number of reasons for automating and provided some possible use cases for quick wins. Take the lead, and show the rest of your team that automation is not a limitation but a force multiplier that will help you all become better analysts.

CHAPTER 8

Real SOC Analyst Stories

In this chapter we will hear a few stories from people on the front lines: their backgrounds, how they landed their first role, and what advice they have for you. These are people from various backgrounds who know they have something important to share. They have blazed this trail and created a path for you to follow. So, enjoy their tale as they take you along their journey.

Kaylil Davis, SOC Analyst

My name is Kaylil Davis, and I am a 21-year-old security analyst with 2 years of experience. My journey has been very unorthodox compared to other security professionals. I have a high-school diploma, no college degree, and no certifications. I have not been coding since my early teens, I am not some sort of computer genius, and I definitely do not know everything there is to know about cybersecurity. The truth is I am just now learning how to code and gaining a better understanding of computers through the Harvard CS50 course and other free resources. So, how did I become a SOC analyst?

© Tyler Wall and Jarrett Rodrick 2021
T. Wall and J. Rodrick, *Jump-start Your SOC Analyst Career*,
https://doi.org/10.1007/978-1-4842-6904-6_8

When I was about 12, I would play my favorite game, *Call of Duty 4: Modern Warfare*, every day after school. One day, I joined a game where the other players were flying, teleporting, and they had all the gear you could possibly get in the game. The players were hackers! This was the first time I had witnessed hacking, and it blew my mind. I wanted to know exactly how they did it, so I watched a lot of videos and browsed the Internet for answers. I eventually came across a site that allowed you to download these "hacks" to a USB and format them for use with your console. I had a blast. Then I learned how to traverse the Windows command line. Whenever I had friends over, I'd open the CLI and type "Color A" and spam "tree" to make it look like I was actually doing something interesting. Needless to say, my mother's laptop paid dearly for my early adventures in hacking. To this day, she has no clue why her laptop was extremely slow and had software on it that she didn't use. (Sorry, Mom.) These experiences sparked my interest in computers.

I initially wanted to become a web developer. During my senior year of high school, I taught myself HTML, CSS, and some basic SQL and was going to begin learning JavaScript. However, that's when I realized I did not like anything I was doing. I didn't like designing websites, and I didn't like practicing code all day. So I researched careers and found out about cybersecurity, which is what I ended up pursuing in college.

College was extremely rough for me. I definitely was not ready for it. I'd highly recommend making sure you form good study and scheduling habits. I had neither and only wanted to do things I was interested in. I didn't want to do electives or anything, just all IT classes. However, as we all know, that's not how college works. You have due dates, assignments, and a one-dimensional learning style in classrooms.

I am also a hands-on learner, which made college even more difficult for me. I believe less than 25% of what I did in school was hands-on learning, and the rest of the time was taken up by PowerPoint slides and reading books.

Here's a tip: if you intend to work in cybersecurity, I suggest you major in any other IT-related field and then pivot to cybersecurity later on. If I could do it all over again, I would do a network engineering degree or CS degree, get work experience, specialize, and then pivot into an infosec role where my skills would transfer nicely and the learning curve would not be so steep. Though a degree in cybersecurity is not useless, the field itself requires one to have a specialty and a certain skill set for a chosen job. Experience is king in infosec and will trump having certs and a degree. With that being said although it does happen, a cybersecurity degree alone probably will not land you a job. During my second year of college, I attended a career fair hosted by my community college, and I landed a security analyst internship with Duke University. When I started the internship, reality hit very hard. Most of what I learned in class was not actually applicable to what I was doing in the real world. I didn't know what a SIEM was (if you don't know, Google it right now!), and most days I had no clue what I was looking at. However, the on-the-job training was very good, and after a few months, I had developed keen eye for spotting phishing emails and suspicious activity in logs.

Around this time, I dropped out of college for personal reasons, but that didn't stop me from continuing my education. This brings me to my next tip: never stop learning. A huge part of working in IT and especially in cybersecurity is personal growth. If you want to be successful in this field, when you get off work, don't go home and do nothing. Go home and pick up the basics of a new skill. Learn how to navigate in Linux, learn how to script in Python, dabble in pen testing to understand how some attacks work, and ask other professionals questions. Asking questions can get you farther than trying to do everything on your own.

A great way to make connections is to create a LinkedIn account and reach out to people in your field. Ask them questions about resources for learning and job responsibilities. From that alone I learned about Linux CTFs, TryHackMe, free certification study resources such as Professor Messer, and more.

After 1 year as an intern and gaining experience at work and doing my personal projects, I started applying for jobs. I landed about eight interviews but found out something important. Job interviews are technical, and you will be tested on whatever you put on your resume. If you have it on your resume, make sure you actually know what you are talking about because they will grill you on that subject. If you don't know something, then admit it, ask for the answer, and ask for an explanation. This shows that you are not only honest, but willing to learn. After each interview, I went back and reviewed the questions I didn't have the answer to. I had about eight interviews and didn't land even the ones I felt like I did well in but continued.

About a year and a half into my internship, I received a call from a recruiter about a junior security analyst position. I jumped at the chance. I came in with confidence, when they asked about certain tech I didn't have experience with, I told them I didn't know much but I would be willing to learn, and for the skills I already have, I would further improve. I got the job.

Now, I'm at a place in my life that still seems unbelievable. My team is very helpful and amazing, I'm starting school again for a degree in cybersecurity, and I'm also studying for my Security+ certification. The journey was full of self-growth, and there were times where I wanted to give up and I felt like I had impostor syndrome, but I kept going. I was determined to grow my career and beat the odds.

My career as a security analyst now has been frustrating and rewarding at the same time. There are some days where you are sitting in front of the screen reading all this data, trying to make something of it but nothing is clicking. You can be researching for almost an hour straight before you find something to run on. For example, I ran into a malware event known as DoublePulsar, and I did not have the slightest idea of what it was, how to find it, or how to prevent it. I researched for a while reading what I could about it so I would understand and be able to effectively report on it. This is a common occurrence. In the end it's always worth it.

The next step in my career will be to get more advanced in my analyst role while learning more about pen testing. Eventually, I make the career transition to pen testing. I feel like my analyst skills would transfer over smoothly, and that's exactly where I belong. It's the exact career that the younger me would have definitely strived for if I knew it existed.

What contributed to my success is my passion for cybersecurity and the amount of time I am willing to dedicate to it so I can succeed. I'm not driven by the monetary aspect or the cool job title. I'm driven by the fact that my career encourages curiosity and allows me to constantly evolve.

My advice to anyone just starting out is to let your mind go and learn more about anything that catches your interest – how to perform an SQL injection, Social Engineering 101, read books on subjects that interest you. If you currently are not working as a security analyst, build the skills yourself and prove that you can. Learn how to use a SIEM, configure a network using GNS3, spin up some VMs, learn Linux by doing CTFs, play with Kali, do anything that shows you have potential. You can never go wrong with personal projects. It's harder than it sounds, but trust me I know if you really want it, you will do it. I'm not that much different from you, and you me.

So I know you can.

Toryana Jones, SOC Analyst

My cybersecurity journey began at Augusta University in 2015. Initially, I enrolled in college with a major in psychology, but shortly after attending orientation, I made the switch to information technology. While pursuing my degree, I worked as an IT support specialist at the help desk on-campus where I performed installation support on end-user environments - including personal computers and peripherals. I learned a lot from that role; it increased my understanding of the differences between devices and applications used by them.

One day while at work, I noticed a few unfamiliar faces and found out that the Cyber Georgia Conference was being held at the university in partnership with the Georgia Chamber of Commerce. Cybersecurity professionals from all over the world were attending the conference to learn and network – it was amazing to see. Hence, my introduction to cybersecurity began! After work, I decided to attend a keynote speaker and panel discussion about the various aspects of cybersecurity. I was able to network with prominent professionals in the community and at my university. The conference was extraordinary, and by the end of it, I decided to pursue a career in cybersecurity. Little did I know, Augusta University had recently announced the Cyber Institute and had open enrollment.

Enrolling in the Cyber Institute to specialize in cybersecurity was one of the best decisions I have made for my career. I volunteered as a Student Mentor for Girls Who Code, where I was tasked with assisting young girls with developing web pages through HTML, CSS, and JavaScript. This opportunity allowed me to expand on my understanding of source code and taught me how to simplify and explain intricate topics.

During the summer of 2017, I volunteered as a Camp Counselor for GenCyber. GenCyber is a 7-day, residential summer camp that is sponsored by the National Security Agency and National Science Foundation. I loved every second of camp and the experience; it gave me an increasing interest in cybersecurity careers and diversity in the nation's workforce.

Through the Cyber Institute at Augusta University, I was able to attend conferences such as Hacker Halted, BSides Augusta, and Women in Cybersecurity (WiCyS). I enjoyed cyber conferences so much that I volunteered at BSides Augusta to bring more visibility to the program. During my senior year of college, I was fortunate to attend WiCyS in Chicago, Illinois, where I met so many amazing people in the industry and learned something new with every keynote speaker. While attending the conference I interviewed with several companies, here are some of the interview questions that were difficult at this time of my career:

- What is the difference between signature-based detection and behavior-based detection?

- What port does ping work over?

- What are the differences between cybersecurity in the cloud and on premises?

- What is the OSI model and how might it be used in your position in this role?

In 2019, I secured a position as a SOC analyst for WarnerMedia. Through the interview process, I was able to determine that the SOC was a team environment that genuinely enjoyed their work, and I could not wait to be a part of it! My first day in the SOC involved training on tools, playbooks, documentation process for tickets, and reviewing findings with other analysts on the team.

Since joining the SOC last year, I have matured greatly in my role. I have had opportunities to train new analysts and interns on the team. I played a role in improving and enhancing security playbooks, which ensure our analysts are responding to security threats in the most efficient and effective way possible. One of my favorite contributions to the SOC so far was scripting and producing an informative and entertaining video on one of the many tactics hackers use to gain access to networks. I look forward to continuing my journey with the SOC and have gained a wealth of knowledge in my first year!

Brandon Glandt, SOC Analyst

Never in my life would I have thought I would finish my undergrad career in the middle of a global pandemic. After being laid off twice within 6 months and not being able to walk across the stage to accept my diploma, I was not sure what was next for me.

During my undergrad career, I studied computer science and economics at CU Boulder. I was also involved in a professional and personal development club known as Silver Wings Society. This organization partnered civilians with our campuses Air Force ROTC to promote military awareness, national defense, and professional development. The idea was that at some point in our careers, civilians and military personnel would most likely work together, so this organization helped bridge that gap a little more.

As professional development organization, they offered scholarships and internships for members. There was only one internship that fit in the broad category of computer science. The internship was for a SOC analyst at a cybersecurity startup in the DC Metro Area. This was the most competitive internship offered through the organization, where only 3 students get selected from nearly 40 different universities. My immediate thought was that I most likely would not get the opportunity because it's very competitive. I decided to apply anyway, because the worst thing that could happen is they say no, so what did I have to lose? All I had to do was send them my resume. Within 24 hours I received an email from the VP of Cyber Operations asking to set up a phone interview. At this point, I was shocked, but also excited. This had told me that they saw something on my resume that they were interested in and caught their eye. We set up the phone interview for that week. Before the interview I was a little nervous; I had no previous experience or knowledge with cybersecurity. That week I had prepared for the interview by teaching myself the basics of cybersecurity and learning about the company itself including their mission and goals. By the time it came to the interview, I was not too nervous. They knew and I knew that I had no prior experience in cybersecurity, and I planned on being honest with them. Before this I had felt a little lost in my degree. With computer science being as broad as it is, I was not sure what I wanted to do with it exactly, but I wanted to continue learning and dive headfirst into something new. The interview ended up not being so much an interview, but just a great conversation. I was offered the internship that day.

Just a few months later in May of 2019, I hopped in my car and drove 24 hours from Denver to Washington DC. Over that summer my love for cybersecurity grew immensely. I learned a lot from being a threat hunter, to familiarizing myself with network and security tools. By the time the summer came to an end, I had built a life in DC, with friends and now a career path to work toward. Silver Wings was the perfect introduction to this company for multiple reasons but especially bridging the gap between civilians and military personnel. The entire C-Suite of executives was filled with retired military, the CEO was the former director of the NSA and the USCYBER COMMAND, and the company was full with people who formally worked for the NSA, the DoD, and the military. As a college student, I thought this was so cool and fascinating to be surrounded by different people from all different walks of life! Being in the cybersecurity industry, being able to communicate and work with colleagues from the government or military was extremely helpful. By the end of the summer, all the interns had to present their own personal projects in front of the entire C-Suite. As an upcoming senior in college, this was such an amazing experience to be able to say I have presented my own project that I completed at an internship to the C-Suite Board. The next step was to come back as a full-time employee after I graduate. But with three semesters away from graduation, nothing was promised.

My senior year was the craziest year of my life. I was trying to graduate in May of 2020 with a few extra classes to take over that summer. I was also now President of Silver Wings at CU Boulder, all while working full-time as a server at the Hilton in town. As President of Silver Wings, our organization was not handed to me in the best condition. We were losing members and at risk of losing our chapter if we could not find more members. When I took over as President, we immediately started recruiting and fundraising.

Spring semester was going great, seniors were planning graduation, and Silver Wings was getting ready to attend our National Conclave in Las Vegas. Within the first 2 weeks in March of 2020, all classes had gone online for the rest of the semester, and I was laid off from the hotel. The coronavirus had hit the entire planet, and everyone was shutting down and social distancing. Overnight, the world had stopped. Over the next few weeks, I was not sure what was going to happen with graduation and finding a job out of college, especially for someone who technically would not graduate until August of 2020. So, I went straight to LinkedIn to ask around for any advice. I had asked my connections on LinkedIn what someone in my situation should do. Shortly after, my old team lead from my internship reached out to me. They saw that I was laid off due to COVID-19, and they wanted to help. Within a month I was now working as a part-time internal SOC analyst with the company. I felt so grateful that they were willing to help me out through these hard times and get back to what I wanted to do, even before graduation. The plan was to work part-time until I graduated and then continue with them full-time. Things were looking good running up to the summer.

At the beginning of the school year, we had eight members, the minimum to stay active. By the time I handed our chapter off to the next president, we were sitting at over 20 members. By May, we were in what we thought was the heat of COVID-19, and my graduation was going to be virtual. I "walked" across a virtual stage and was awarded the Silver Wings Chapter President of the Year Award.

With only 8 weeks of summer classes to go, things seemed to be going as well as they could. A few weeks in, my manager called. The company had to unfortunately lay off employees due to COVID-19. This was the second time I had been laid off due to COVID-19 in less than 5 months. Never in my life would I have thought to see a world pandemic, nor to be laid off once or twice! The economy during my college career was growing exponentially, and college graduates were looking at plenty of open job positions. The class of 2020 was looking at the worst economy for jobs since the great depression. I decided to focus on my last few weeks of undergrad and apply to jobs as I go. I was not special nor was I the only one experiencing hardships during this time.

August 2020 came faster than I could have thought. I had officially graduated college! It was not how I expected college graduation to be, but no one could take it away from me. The next step was finding a job. I had been applying to probably hundreds of jobs when I was not in class or studying. I probably heard back from 3 or 4, whether they were looking to set up the next step, or let me know that the position had been filled. I started changing where and how I was applying for jobs, so I began to look at different recruiting agencies. One day I got a call from a recruiter, telling me that he had a job position open for me over at Darktrace, and it looks like I fit the bill. We met countless times either preparing for the interviews or making sure I was what Darktrace was looking for. I had made it to the final interview round after a month-long process. During all of this, I continued my job search elsewhere and stumbled upon a company named Nuspire in Denver. In the middle of the interviews for Darktrace, I was also interviewing with Nuspire, where I had also made it to the final round of interviews in only a short few weeks.

I preferred the job with Nuspire because it was something new and would be a larger learning curve for me, although I would clearly be happy with either job. After I had completed the final interview for each company, I was waiting eagerly. After about a week, I had gotten a call, making me the newest SOC analyst at Nuspire in Denver. I immediately had accepted because it was my first choice and could not have been more thrilled and excited.

Clearly this is not your typical college graduate job-seeking story, but who's really is? My story is unique, and I learned a lot throughout the way. Throughout college I am so glad I tried to be as active as I could while participating in Silver Wings, attending school full-time, and working a full-time job. I cannot tell you how many friends I tried to recruit to Silver

Wings just so they can have access to scholarships and internships. The only thing they had to lose was a small yearly membership fee. But a lot of my friends missed out on great internships that could probably help them find a job right now. Connections is a huge part of it as well. Those connections they could have made could have helped them through so many ways throughout their careers. Take my story, for example, if I never would have applied for that internship, I would have been unemployed for an additional 3 months and would not have those extra months of experience on my resume. I highly encourage everyone to just say yes and try new things, even if you may not be sure about it or think you will receive it, the worst thing that could happen is you stay exactly where you are. I cannot express connections enough. These are just a few things I have learned throughout my journey to get where I currently am.

If I could give someone advice whether they are in a similar position to where I was or in an entirely different position, it is to do as much as you can. Join that club, even if you end up not going to every meeting. Apply for that scholarship, even if it's only for a few hundred dollars. Send your resume for that job or internship that maybe you are not qualified for; what do you have to lose? I am sure we have all heard this saying before, but you miss every shot you do not take.

This is only the beginning of my story, and I am only going up from here. As a current SOC analyst, I am also studying to take the Security+ certification exam soon and then from there the Network+ Exam as well. In the future I hope to learn as much as I can while becoming familiar in the industry. One day I hope to protect travel companies whether it is the hotel industry, airline industry, or the cruise industry, and be a leader in the community.

Matthew Arias, SOC Analyst

My name is Matthew Arias and I am currently a tier 3 SOC analyst. I currently have 11 certifications and no formal college degree. I have spent 10 years of my time as an IT in the Navy and have done everything from tier 1-3 trouble ticket resolution to tech refreshes, server installs, GPO implementation, and domain integration, as well as vulnerability compliance, reporting, and more. I really got my break the last 3.5 years in the Navy where I worked for a cyber protection team. There, I learned how to conduct computer network exploitation, create shellcode, learned a bit of assembly, digital forensics, and network traffic analysis. This would all come together during my deployments to Central and South America during incident response engagements. I am blessed to have worked there in the capacity I did where I received exposure and knowledge to tools I would later use, such as Splunk, Kibana, Tanium, Security Onion, Bro/Zeek, and Wireshark.

I have always had an interest in cybersecurity and technology as a whole ever since I was young. I fondly remember my first experience with a computer around age 10, where I found an old Apple computer in a box. It was not connected nor plugged in, and I spent several hours connecting the PS/2 connections, power cord, and VGA cable to make it all work. In hindsight it was really a 1-minute job, but back then that kind of technology was foreign. I used to play this maze game religiously on it and write random notes in the notepad. This was a very defining moment for me, and the moment I know now where my curiosity in technology began. That curiosity continued through my teen years where my friends would play pranks with each other using trojans to move the mouse erratically or open the CD drive on the PC. I would frequently visit Yahoo chatrooms and learned about "booters," applications that overloaded Yahoo chat clients with smiley faces or ascii characters and kicked you offline. I learned how to program with

Visual Basic 6 and made my own custom booters, as well as account lockers (attempting the wrong password several times locked accounts out). At this point, I really considered becoming a programmer, as there are no two equal approaches and only infinite ways to accomplish a single task. This all changed at age 17, where I downloaded pirated software that was flagged as a trojan. I was really upset that I was almost "tricked" and almost became a victim. Before this, I had learned a bit about reverse engineering applications and decompiling them. This is how I found an FTP username and password and realized that the attacker was sending stolen credentials from victims to his FTP server. I logged into the FTP with the credentials and found hundreds of gigabytes of text files, each with numerous credentials, from email addresses to bank account logins and more. This was a heavy weight on me at the time, as I was complicit for logging in without authorization into an FTP server. I decided to do what I felt was right and deleted all the text files from the server. I have no doubt I saved thousands of people the headache of dealing with fraudulent charges, stolen money, and much more.

My time in the Navy was very exciting and rewarding, and I loved that no two days were ever the same, and I never knew what I would be doing the next day. Unfortunately, that was part of the problem as I grew older, and I wanted a sense of stability. Moving almost every 3-4 years was not conductive to my newfound goal, and it really felt like I was starting life all over again with every move.

Then, an opportunity landed in my lap, thanks to Tim Cookson. He was a coworker of mine in the Navy who had gotten out several months before me and was approached with a job offer as a SOC analyst. He knew I was getting out and told the recruiter he would only accept their offer if they hired me. A little bit about our relationship: He was a CTR in the Navy and dealt with radio communications. He was not familiar with cybersecurity or IT at all. We worked together, and he learned from me via osmosis and being on deployments, he got hands-on experience. He learned extremely quick and was outpacing some coworkers in my field by a lot. To this day he credits most of his skills and knowledge to me, but I would disagree. He would spend all of his off time dedicated to going to UMUC college classes to learn more, stay up late building labs and playing around, and always going out of his way off hours to get engaged with what us analysts were doing. He felt he owed me something, and that was getting me a job. I interviewed with several people and they wanted to hire us. We accepted.

My first day in the SOC was kind of rough. There was no rank structure, everyone was on the same "playing field" for the most part, and civilian life seemed kind of chaotic. I didn't know how to properly address people such as the VP of the company. I just kind of stayed quiet and gauged how everyone else was communicating among themselves. It was the longest 8 hours of my life, and I definitely felt awkward. I picked up my hardware and laptop and sat down with other SOC analysts so they could assist me in getting my email and Citrix environment situated. Everyone was very quiet and responded as directly as possible to me, even when I tried to get more personal with them. Come to find out, one of the analysts ask me if I was their new boss, and suddenly I realized why everyone was afraid of me. I was dressed to the nines in a suit and tie in a very casual environment, and I think that threw them off as the only people who visit in suits are very high executives from our clients.

I have done several interviews before accepting that job, as well as numerous interviews since, and there are several things to keep in mind when it comes to recruiting. We focus so much in the cyber/IT field on technical ability when in reality that accounts for probably half of what companies are looking for. Above all, anyone interviewing you is trying to gauge whether you'd fit culturally into the team. They want to hear your reaction to very specific events or may ask you to expand on parts of your experience. They want to understand how you work, and if you will work well with their team. Be genuine in this respect, and be completely honest, especially if you do not have or know the answer. Make sure you highlight your accomplishments during an interview, and as much as possible, tie that into how it would benefit the company. Going from an incident handler to a SOC analyst, I stated that I understand the incident response life cycle and would integrate well as a tier 3 SOC analyst with the understanding of how our incident handlers would work to resolve intrusions, as well as having relevant experience doing so. Lastly, remember that you are interviewing them as much as they are you. I don't like to talk to recruiters or hiring managers about day-to-day and usually request to speak to a junior or midlevel analyst. How they are treated and how heavily involved they are within tier 2 and tier 3 endeavors speak volumes about the climate of the company. They usually give you a raw and unfiltered perspective on what you will most likely be doing.

Knowing what I know now, I wish I would have left my ego at the door. I would have made magnitudes of progress had I stopped comparing or talking and just listened. Even the most junior analyst had come across, read or understands a concept that you can learn from. I believe this ultimately stems from what is known as "impostor syndrome," which is a feeling or inclination that you are not as good as you are. Almost everyone I have come across has experienced it to some degree, and I believe the need to "prove" myself has sheltered me from the thoughts and ideas of others. Another thing I wish I had done was demonstrate all my skills, even the ones beyond cybersecurity such as programming, in a way I could share with future employers and also help the community. Things such as offering free classes to teach either adults looking to transition into the field or teens wanting to learn or assist in some capacity to a GitHub project. This would show others that this is a passion and also allow you to network with others. As far as certifications go, I would place more emphasis on quality not quantity. CompTIA certifications are good, but they are not viewed as heavily as SANS, ISC2, or ISACA certifications. This matters as most job postings will have CISSP or GCIH listed many times more than Security+ is.

Being in a SOC usually means a 24x7x365 environment. With that said, you have to be OK with a somewhat sporadic schedule especially if you are low on manning, or have shift changes every week/month/quarter. You will also need to sometimes sacrifice weekends and free time if someone calls out or a breach has occurred. This makes life a little hard to plan around, especially if the SOC is not fully matured and autonomous. Lastly, I wish I had finished college. I am currently trying to wrap up my Associates, but I put so much emphasis on certifications that I do not have any formal education. In the cybersecurity field, it is not inherently damaging to not have college education, but I have been passed up for promotion to management position simply for not having it. Hopefully that will not happen again.

Although I have enjoyed creating a SOC environment from the ground up and enjoy responding to incidents, I am slowly transitioning into becoming a penetration tester. It is a whole new field which requires a completely different skill set, one where understanding things as a computer would is critical. I have been subject to penetration tests and performed in a blue team capacity to determine entry point and scope of breach, but I want to learn more about exploitation. I am currently doing Hack the Box labs in my free time and utilizing Metasploit on my home lab. I hope the transition is quick and painless, although so far I am learning something new every day!

Rebecca Blair, SOC Director

Throughout my career, working in SOC environments has by far been the best time. There is always a level of camaraderie that you make with the other people that are triaging with you. Personally, I always get an adrenaline rush when investigating a large-scale incident. It was the excitement that you were the one, or part of the team, that was going to figure out this puzzle, and from there have a large direct impact on the organization that you work for.

Looking back, from the time when I was just starting out to making it to the director of SOC operations roles, I don't have any regrets because it has led me to where I am today, but there is plenty of advice that I wish I could give myself. First when starting off a career in a SOC, be humble. I know personally out of college, I thought I knew it all, and the reality is it's impossible to know it all because the world of cyber is ever changing. I would walk into the certifications exams, having not studied, and while I was fortunate that I passed, I could not recommend ever doing that. I wish had continued learning outside of work. While in college, I would compete in Capture-the-Flag exercises, and was constantly learning; however, when I first entered the workforce, I didn't continue with that trend. Eventually after a few years I realized the importance of always learning, and started to set up the home labs, and get more involved in the infosec community. I also wish I understood the balance of work and life. I was a workaholic, and admittedly still can be, but being fatigued from looking at too many alerts is a real thing, and when it happens, you are more likely to incorrectly rate, or triage an alert.

The next thing that I wish I knew was that every day was going to be different. When working in a SOC, you have to become a jack-of-all-trades, because you are typically looking at both host-based and network logs, and are expected to have a wide range of knowledge to be able to effectively triage. I didn't initially realize that no two days would ever be the same, and in reality that is what I like the most about working in SOC environments.

Finally, the last thing that I wish I knew, and recently learned, is the concept of assuming goodwill. Essentially that means that when you come across an alert for a user that might not look good, don't automatically assume that they are intentionally malicious. There have been more alerts/ incidents than I can count that have been the result from someone who didn't realize they clicked on a link, or honestly thought it was legitimate. One time, there was a company-wide phishing test, and in the phishing email was a link to a spreadsheet for everyone to sign up for a potluck.

One employee repeatedly tried to open the spreadsheet so they could sign up for the potluck, and took a lot of convincing to understand that the sheet was actually malicious. So, that is why earlier in my career, I wished I had assumed goodwill rather than jumping to conclusions, and thinking that everyone was an inside actor trying to compromise our network. In fairness, there are cases of that as well. I've fortunately, or unfortunately depending on how you view it, have taken part in many large-scale incident response efforts. Relatively early on in my career, I received a call from my boss, stating that I had to report to the office over the weekend. When I showed up on Saturday, I was briefed that 11 servers had been publicly accessible for years, and that we had to conduct log analysis for all of the servers, and had to review logs for every year that they were accessible. At the time, the company I worked for was as a subcontractor to a larger contractor/organization, so the entire team to look through these logs consisted of only a few of us. I think if you add all of the times that I have used Grep commands since that day, it still wouldn't match the amount that I used it that weekend.

Other instances in my career were learning about the unfortunate reality that so many organizations have software that is end of life, because they don't have the budget space to upgrade the software. One of my first large-scale incidents that involved customers was when a company that provided endpoint detection software had a setting automatically enabled where they would send files from the endpoints up to VirusTotal to be reviewed for legitimacy. The kicker is that anyone who has a professional account to VirusTotal can access any file that has been uploaded to them for review, which, by itself, can be helpful for malware analysis; however, it is not helpful when a customer contacts your organization and says that they saw some of their information that our company had uploaded to VirusTotal. This led to an over month-long investigation, to determine the entire scope of how many files were uploaded and what they contained. We also had to work with VirusTotal to get the files removed. On top of all of that, we had to work with the endpoint company to disable that "feature." Another larger-scale incident was a few years ago when a user, who was a contractor, was found to be contracting out their work. Initially the user was reported for trying to install software that was against the company's acceptable use policy. After counseling the user, we thought everything was good. About a month later, we noticed odd timestamps, and multifactor authentication pushes being accepted from an area that that user was not living. Through a lot of traffic and log analysis, we had built a comprehensive timeline and file that proved the contractor had given their credentials to a third-party group, which was then completing their work. The contractor was of course terminated from their contract.

While these are some instances of larger-scale incidents that I have been fortunate to have the opportunity to work, they are few and far between. You are much more likely to work incident response on an end user clicking a phishing link, or downloading a potentially unwanted program. That's why you need to be constantly training and learning, so that when a large incident does happen, you are ready. For anyone looking to enter the world of the SOC, remember this, keep learning and training, always work to put all of the pieces of the puzzle together, and have fun with it; the best SOC analysts have a passion for this type of work.

Summary

As the alarm sounds, your consciousness is brought to attention for a brand new day. You take a cold shower this morning to be extra alert. You're already energized, but make a cup of coffee anyway. You're ready to start your new life as a SOC analyst as you plop down in your perfectly positioned swivel chair letting it bounce for a split second. You swivel around to your desk, staring at the monitor at eye level, and then you take your first sip of coffee for the morning, letting the stimulating aroma arouse your mind. You close your eyes to enjoy the moment. You bask in the incredible accomplishment of getting your career on track. You say "ahhhh" as this feeling is exactly how you've imagined it. You worked hard to get here so you just take a moment to enjoy the experience of life. The feeling is extremely rewarding, and after you enjoyed every second and it is gone, you start your first day with my advice to remember to ask questions and stay curious. There are themes that echo from great SOC analysts, and Walt Disney said it the best:

> *Around here, however, we don't look backwards for very long. We keep moving forward, opening up new doors and doing new things, because we're curious . . . and curiosity keeps leading us down new paths.*

> —Walt Disney

Index

A

Access control lists (ACLs), 43
Acme Brick Company (ABC), 48
Address space layout
        randomization (ASLR), 48
Application security, 75, 76
Arias, Matthew, 101–105
Auditor teams, 22
Availability, 43
AWS Elastic Beanstalk, 69
AWS Redshift, 69
Azure App Service, 69

B

Blair, Rebecca, 105–108
BSides, 29, 94

C

Chief Information Security
        Officer (CISO), 17
Chromebook, 52
Cloud computing, 65
    types, 67
    vs. traditional computing, 65
Cloud Foundry, 69

Cloud management platform
        (CMP), 67, 68
Cloud security, 14, 16, 73–75
Cloud service models, 68, 69
Command and Control (C2), 4
Cryptography, 44, 45
C-Suite, 97
Cybersecurity analyst, 1, 3–5, 10, 21
Cybersecurity incident, 4
Cybersecurity professionals, 8
Cybersecurity workers, 1
Cybersecurity workforce, 2, 3

D

Database as a Service (DBaaS), 69
Data Warehouse as a Service
        (DWaaS), 69
Davis, Kaylil, 89–93
Defcon conference, 28
Defense Industrial Base
        Cybersecurity (DIB CS), 21
Department of
        Defense (DoD), 22, 37
Department of Homeland Security
        (DHS), 1, 21
Desktop as a Service (DaaS), 69

© Tyler Wall and Jarrett Rodrick 2021
T. Wall and J. Rodrick, *Jump-start Your SOC Analyst Career*,
https://doi.org/10.1007/978-1-4842-6904-6

Made in United States
North Haven, CT
10 September 2023

41366204R00076